The Complete Fishing Guide

Everything From the Basics to Incredible Fishing Stories

Regan Murphy

© **Copyright 2024 - All rights reserved.**

The content contained within this book may not be reproduced, duplicated or transmitted without direct written permission from the author or the publisher.

Under no circumstances will any blame or legal responsibility be held against the publisher, or author, for any damages, reparation, or monetary loss due to the information contained within this book, either directly or indirectly.

Legal Notice:

This book is copyright protected. It is only for personal use. You cannot amend, distribute, sell, use, quote or paraphrase any part, or the content within this book, without the consent of the author or publisher.

Disclaimer Notice:

Please note the information contained within this document is for educational and entertainment purposes only. All effort has been executed to present accurate, up to date, reliable, complete information. No warranties of any kind are declared or implied. Readers acknowledge that the author is not engaged in the rendering of legal, financial, medical or professional advice. The content within this book has been derived from various sources. Please consult a licensed professional before attempting any techniques outlined in this book.

By reading this document, the reader agrees that under no circumstances is the author responsible for any losses, direct or indirect, that are incurred as a result of the use of the information contained within this document, including, but not limited to, errors, omissions, or inaccuracies.

Table of Contents

INTRODUCTION 1

CHAPTER 1: THE BASICS—ESSENTIAL SKILLS 5
    FISHING LICENSE AND REGULATIONS 6
    FISHING GEAR 7
        Fishing Rod 8
        Reel 9
        Fishing Line 10
    HOOKS, BAITS, AND LURES 11
        Hooks 12
        Baits 13
        Lures 15
    KNOT TYING 17
    CASTING TECHNIQUES 18
    HOOK SETTING 20
    FISHING LOCATIONS 21
    PATIENCE 23
    FISH HANDLING AND SAFETY 24
        Fish Handling 25
        Safety 26
    WEATHER AWARENESS AND ENVIRONMENTAL RESPECT 27
    WEATHER INTERPRETATION 28
    FISH IDENTIFICATION TIPS 29
    WATERCRAFT NAVIGATION 31
    NIGHT FISHING 32
    SAFETY MEASURES 34
    FISH CLEANING AND FILLETING 35
    FISH FINDING TECHNOLOGY 36
    DEEP SEA FISHING 38

CHAPTER 2: IDENTIFYING FISH AND WHERE TO FIND THEM 41
    FISH SPECIES IDENTIFICATION 42
        Importance of Recognizing Various Fish Species 43
        Distinctive Markings and Characteristics 44
        Examples of Common Fish Species 46
    BEHAVIORAL SIGNATURES 46
        Understanding Species-Specific Behaviors 46

Observing Schooling Patterns *48*
Analyzing Feeding Behaviors *49*
HABITAT PREFERENCES 51
Importance of Habitat in Fish Distribution *51*
Identifying Prime Locations *53*
Examples of Ideal Habitats for Different Species *54*
SEASONAL MIGRATIONS 55
Following Seasonal Patterns *56*
Spawning Seasons and Migration Routes *57*
Impact on Fishing Strategies *58*
WATER TEMPERATURE AND CONDITIONS 60
Influence of Water Temperature on Fish Behavior *60*
Understanding Water Clarity and Oxygen Levels *62*
Identifying Productive Fishing Spots Based on Conditions *63*
RIVER FISHING STRATEGIES 64
Dynamics of River Environments *65*
Locating Fish in Varying Currents *66*
Strategies for Changing Conditions *67*
LAKE AND POND TACTICS 69
Diverse Habitats in Lakes and Ponds *69*
Targeting Fish in Shoreline Structures and Deep Basins *70*
SALTWATER HOTSPOTS 71
Exploring the Vastness of the Ocean *72*
Understanding Tidal Movements and Coastal Structures *73*
OFFSHORE ADVENTURES FOR SALTWATER ANGLING 74

CHAPTER 3: FLY FISHING **77**

THE FLY FISHING EXPERIENCE 78
Fly Fishing as a Holistic Pursuit *78*
The Angler, the Fly, and the Environment *79*
Rhythmic Casting and Anticipation *79*
PHILOSOPHY OF THE SPORT 80
Understanding the Fly *80*
The Art of Fly Tying *81*
Selecting the Right Fly Patterns *81*
Matching the Hatch *82*
CASTING AS AN ART FORM 84
Overhead Cast *85*
Double Haul *86*
Dry Fly Presentation vs. Double Haul *86*
READING THE WATER FOR FLY FISHING 87
Deciphering the Currents *87*
Identifying Feeding Lanes *88*
Understanding Water Flow *89*

PRESENTATION AND DRIFT CONTROL 90
   Achieving a Natural Drift..90
   Subtleties of Presentation 91
   Mending Line and Controlling Drift 92
MOUNTAIN STREAMS AND CREEKS 92
   Stealth and Precision 93
   Pursuing Native Trout..93
   Challenges and Rewards 94
STILLWATER FLY FISHING 95
   Strategies for Enticing Cruising Trout..96
   Adapting to Open Waters..97
SALTWATER FLY FISHING 98
   Extending Fly Fishing to Coastal Flats 99
   Encounter With Saltwater Species..100
   Adapting to Tides and Currents...101

CHAPTER 4: FISH PREPARATION, FILLETING, AND STEAKING........................103

GEARING UP 104
   Essential Tools for Fish Cleaning, Filleting, and Steaking 104
   Importance of a Sharp Fillet Knife and Clean Workspace.......................105
SAFETY FIRST 106
   Knife-Handling Techniques..106
   Nonslip Cutting Board 107
   Controlled Environment..108
   Safety Measures to Avoid Accidents...109
SCALING THE FISH 109
GUTTING THE FISH 112
   Careful Removal of Internal Organs 112
   Avoiding Contamination During the Gutting Process.............................113
TAIL-TO-HEAD FILLET 115
   Techniques for Different Fish Species 117
SKINNING THE FILLET 118
   Skin-On vs. Skinless Fillets 119
   Mastering the Art of Skinning 121
PIN-BONE REMOVAL 122
   Detecting and Removing Pin Bones Effectively 122
   Enhancing the Dining Experience by Eliminating Small Bones 123
STEAKING LARGER FISH 124
   Method for Creating Steaks 125
   Considerations for Different Types of Steaks...126
PORTION CONTROL 127
   Creating Evenly Sized Cuts..127
   Mastering Portioning for Consistent Cooking 129
   Tips for Uniform Fillets and Steaks...130

  Culinary Sustainability 131
    Making Fish Stock... 132
    Creating Fish Bait 133
    Enhancing Sustainability Through Creativity... 134

CHAPTER 5: INCREDIBLE, TRUE, AND SOMETIMES TERRIFYING TALES!............137
  Chasing the World Record Tiger Shark... 138
  The Darwin Trip 143
  A Fishing Trip We Would Rather Forget 156
  The Little Boat That Slayed Goliath 159
  Some Final Sound Bites From the Fishing Legend... 161

CONCLUSION 165

REFERENCES 167
  Image References 168

Introduction

So, you've decided to dip your toes (and hopefully a line or two) into the vast, mysterious world of fishing. Well, my friend, you've just cracked open the ultimate guidebook—*The Complete Fishing Guide*. Trust me, you're in for a reel treat!

Picture this: You, sitting by the tranquil waters, the sun kissing your face, a gentle breeze whispering through the trees, and the anticipation of what might just be the biggest catch of your life swimming beneath the surface. Sounds like the ultimate fishing scenario, doesn't it? Well, grab your hat and tackle box because we're about to dive headfirst into the adventure of a lifetime.

Now, before you start envisioning yourself as the next Hemingway of the fishing world, let me assure you that even the most seasoned anglers had to start somewhere. And that somewhere is right here, within the pages of this book. Whether you're a novice looking to master the basics or a seasoned pro seeking some new tricks, consider this your one-stop shop for all things fishing.

But hey, I promise it's not all technical jargon and fishy business. Nope, we're tossing in a healthy dose of incredible fishing stories too. Because let's face it, half the fun of fishing is swapping tales of the one that got away (or the one you managed to reel in against all odds).

From the serene art of fly fishing to the adrenaline-pumping thrill of deep-sea angling, we're covering it all.

Now, let's address the elephant in the room (or should I say, the trout in the stream?): your fishing woes. Believe me, I get it. We've all been there, standing at the water's edge, scratching our heads and wondering why, oh why, those slippery fish just won't bite. But fear not, my friend, because I've been in the trenches and I know exactly where you're coming from.

First up, let's talk about the dreaded backlash. Ah yes, the bane of every angler's existence. You cast your line with all the finesse of a seasoned pro, only to watch in horror as it snarls into a tangled mess worthy of a sailor's knot. It's enough to make even the most patient fisherman want to hurl their rod into the nearest lake. But fret not, because I'm here to help you conquer the backlash beast once and for all.

And then there's the issue of finding the perfect spot. You spend hours scouring maps, consulting fellow anglers, and maybe even sacrificing a lucky lure to the fishing gods in the hopes of stumbling upon that elusive honey hole. But alas, sometimes it feels like you might as well be searching for Atlantis.

Oh, and let's not forget about the weather. Mother Nature has a wicked sense of humor, doesn't she? One minute it's bright and sunny, the birds are chirping, and you're convinced it's going to be the perfect day for fishing. But then, out of nowhere, a storm rolls in faster than you can say "fish fry," leaving you soaked to the bone and wondering why you ever thought this was a good idea. But, for that, I've got some weatherproofing hacks that'll have you singing in the rain (or at least staying dry while you fish).

And don't even get me started on the one that got away. We've all got a tale to tell about the monster fish that slipped through our fingers at the last possible moment. It's enough to make you want to throw in the towel and take up some other hobby instead.

So, whether you're battling the backlash blues, struggling to find the perfect fishing spot, or just trying to stay dry in the face of Mother Nature's wrath, remember this: you're not alone. We've all been there, we've all wrestled with the same fishing frustrations, and we've all lived to tell the tale.

Now, let's talk about what brought you here in the first place. Sure, the title of this book might have caught your eye, but there's always a deeper reason, isn't there? Maybe you're tired of feeling like a fish out of water every time you cast a line. Perhaps you've had one too many fishing trips end in frustration, and you're ready to turn things around. Or maybe, just maybe, you've got a burning desire to finally out-fish that know-it-all uncle of yours at the family reunion. Hey, we've all got our motivations, and I'm not here to judge.

But whatever it is that sparked that fire in your belly and led you to pick up this book, I want you to know one thing: you're in the right place. So, take a deep breath, crack open these pages, and get ready to embark on the fishing adventure of a lifetime. Because trust me, the only thing bigger than the fish you're going to catch is the smile on your face when you do.

Before we go any further, allow me to introduce myself: I'm Regan Murphy, your go-to guide through the choppy waters of the angling world. Now, you might be wondering, "What makes this gal qualified to teach me a thing or two about fishing?" Well, let me reel you in with a little backstory.

You see, fishing isn't just a hobby for me—it's practically in my DNA. I was born into a family of bona fide fishing fanatics, with a lineage boasting over a century of combined angling experience. Yep, you heard that right—between my old man, my brother, and me, we've spent more time on the water than a school of trout.

Growing up surrounded by seasoned fishermen and a treasure trove of fishy tales passed down through the generations, I couldn't help but become hooked on the sport myself. From the gentle lapping of the waves to the thrill of reeling in a big one, fishing isn't just something I do—it's who I am.

But it's not just my familial ties that make me the perfect person to guide you on your fishing journey. Nope, I've also put in the hours of meticulous research, tapping into the collective wisdom of anglers far and wide. I've combed through the latest techniques, tested out the hottest gear, and even braved a few fishing fiascos of my own—all in the name of helping you become the best angler you can be.

So, if you're ready to dive headfirst into the world of fishing with someone who's got the experience, the passion, and maybe a few fishy tales to share, then look no further. This book isn't just another run-of-the-mill fishing guide—it's your ticket to angling success, delivered with a side of wit, wisdom, and a sprinkle of that special Murphy magic. So, grab your rod, pack your sense of adventure, and let's embark on the ultimate fishing escapade together. Trust me you're in for a whale of a time!

Chapter 1:

The Basics—Essential Skills

Welcome, fellow anglers, to Chapter 1: The Basics—where every great fishing adventure begins! Picture this: you, me, and the open water, armed with nothing but our trusty rods, a bucketful of bait, and a whole lot of enthusiasm. But before we dive headfirst into the deep end (or should I say the deep sea?), let's take a moment to brush up on the essential skills that will set us up for fishing success.

In this chapter, we're going back to basics, my friends. We'll cover everything from obtaining that all-important fishing license to mastering the art of knot tying. And hey, don't worry if you're still struggling to tell your spinners from your crankbaits—I've got you covered. By the time we're through, you'll be casting like a pro, reeling in the big ones with ease, and maybe even giving ol' Captain Ahab a run for his money.

So, grab your gear, strap on your fishing hat, and get ready to embark on the ultimate fishing crash course.

Fishing License and Regulations

Before we go any further, it's crucial to understand the ins and outs of local fishing regulations. Trust me, you don't want to end up on the wrong side of the law—it's not a good look, and the fish won't appreciate it either.

Now, let's talk licenses. No, not the kind you need for driving a boat—though that's a good idea, too—but the ones required to fish legally in your area. Think of it as your golden ticket to angler paradise. Here's the lowdown on what you need to know (*Fishing Licenses and Regulations*, n.d.):

- **State-specific:** First off, where you're fishing matters. Each state has its own set of rules and regulations, so make sure you're up to date with what's required in your neck of the woods.

- **Type of water:** Freshwater or saltwater? Your license choice depends on where you'll be casting your line. Freshwater licenses cover lakes, rivers, and streams, while saltwater licenses are for those salty sea adventures.

- **Purpose and duration:** Are you fishing for fun or planning to sell your catch? Will you be out for just a day or two, or are you in it for the long haul? These factors will influence the type and duration of the license you need.

- **Residency and age:** Are you a local or just passing through? And hey, if you're a seasoned angler or a wide-eyed newbie, there might be discounts or even freebies available based on your age and residency status.

- **Special permits:** Depending on your fishing plans, you might need additional permits or tags. Whether it's for specific species, gear, or fishing in federal waters, it's essential to dot your i's and cross your t's.

- **Federal waters:** Ah, the open ocean beckons! If you're venturing into federal waters, make sure you're squared away with any additional permits required by NOAA Fisheries. And hey, if you're headed to Hawaii, Puerto Rico, or the U.S. Virgin Islands, there are a few extra hoops to jump through.

Before you grab your tackle box and head out on your next fishing expedition, do your homework and make sure you've got all the necessary licenses and permits. It'll save you a world of trouble—and hey, the fish will thank you, too!

Fishing Gear

No fishing adventure is complete without the right tools for the job. From rods to reels and everything in between, we're diving into the wonderful world of fishing gear in this section.

Fishing Rod

Alright, let's talk fishing rods—your trusty companion in the quest for that elusive catch. When it comes to choosing the right rod, it's not just about grabbing the first one you see and hoping for the best. Oh no, my friend, selecting the perfect rod is an art form in itself, and I'm here to guide you through it.

Choosing the Right Rod Type

First things first, let's consider your fishing playground. Are you a freshwater fanatic or a saltwater enthusiast? Maybe you've got a soft spot for fly fishing? Your fishing environment and target species will dictate the type of rod that suits you best.

For those who prefer the serene charm of freshwater lakes and rivers, spinning rods and baitcasting rods are the name of the game. Spinning rods offer versatility and ease of use, perfect for beginners and seasoned pros alike. On the other hand, baitcasting rods provide precision and power, ideal for anglers looking to level up their game (*How to Choose the Right Fishing Rod*, 2023).

If you're setting sail into the salty depths, you'll need a rod that can handle the rough and tumble of ocean life. Saltwater rods are designed to withstand the corrosive nature of the sea and are built tough to tackle larger fish species and unforgiving conditions (*How to Choose the Right Fishing Rod*, 2023).

Now, let's talk technique. Whether you're trolling, jigging, or bottom fishing, there's a rod out there tailored to your needs. From sturdy trolling rods to flexible jigging rods, each specialized rod is crafted to help you master your chosen fishing style (*How to Choose the Right Fishing Rod*, 2023).

Considering Rod Length and Action

Alright, let's size things up! When it comes to rod length, it's all about finding the sweet spot between casting distance, leverage, and control (*How to Choose the Right Fishing Rod*, 2023).

- **Casting distance:** Longer rods offer the advantage of casting further distances, perfect for wide-open spaces like lakes or oceans. But if you're fishing in tight quarters, a shorter rod might be your best bet for maneuverability.

- **Leverage and control:** Longer rods provide increased leverage for wrangling those big fish, while shorter rods offer precision and control in close-quarters combat.

- **Power and action:** Now, let's talk power and action—the dynamic duo of fishing rod characteristics. Think of power as your rod's muscle—it determines how much force it takes to bend that bad boy. From ultra-light to extra-heavy, there's a power rating for every fish species and fishing scenario. Action describes where and how your rod flexes, influencing its sensitivity and responsiveness. Whether you prefer fast, medium, or slow action, there's a rod out there waiting to help you feel every bite and reel in every catch.

So, there you have it—your crash course in fishing rod fundamentals.

Reel

When it comes to the reel, there's a lot to consider. From spool capacities to drag forces, choosing the right reel can make or break your angling experience. So, let's dive right in!

Matching Reel to Rod

Now, when you're browsing the reel aisle, you'll notice that reels come in different sizes, usually denoted by numbers like 100, 200, or 400. But fear not—these numbers aren't just for show—they actually indicate the capacity of the spool. And why does that matter? Well, it all comes down to the size of the fish you're after. Planning to reel in some hefty, muscle-bound fish? You'll want a larger reel that can handle the extra drag force.

Now, let's talk about matching your reel to your rod. It's like finding the perfect fishing buddy—they've gotta be compatible! Pay attention to the strength of your fishing line and make sure your reel can handle it. Check out your rod for the gauge, and pick a reel that can comfortably handle a line of the same strength (HOW TO CHOOSE A FISHING REEL, n.d.). You don't want your line snapping just as you're reeling in the big one!

Selecting Appropriate Reel Type

Alright, now that we've covered the basics, it's time to talk reel types. Spinning, baitcasting, fly reels—oh my! With so many options out there, it can feel a bit overwhelming. But fear not, my friends, I've got a step-by-step guide to help you navigate the reel jungle (Bailey, 2023).

- **Step 1—Start with your goals.** First things first, determine your fishing goals. What kind of fish do you want to catch? What's your preferred fishing environment? And perhaps most importantly, what's your skill level? Whether you're a beginner looking for simplicity or a seasoned pro craving precision, there's a reel out there for you.

- **Step 2—Evaluate the specifications.** Once you've narrowed down your options, it's time to dive into the nitty-gritty details. Check out the line capacity, drag system, gear ratio, and durability of each reel. Make sure it's up to the task of reeling in those trophy catches!

- **Step 3—Budget and brand.** Last but not least, consider your budget and brand preferences. There's a wide range of options out there, from budget-friendly basics to high-end reels. Find the sweet spot that balances cost and quality, and don't forget to look for reputable brands with solid warranties.

Fishing Line

Choosing the right fishing line is vital for success on the water, but with hundreds of options available, it can be overwhelming. Thankfully, understanding your target species, fishing conditions, and preferred techniques can help narrow down your choices. There are three main types of fishing lines: monofilament, braided, and fluorocarbon, each with its unique properties and applications.

Monofilament line: This classic fishing line has been a staple for anglers for decades, offering versatility and ease of use. It's forgiving when fighting fish due to its stretchy nature, making it ideal for beginners and experienced anglers alike. However, its stretch can sometimes hinder sensitivity, and it's prone to line twist, especially in lighter tests (McNally, 2018).

Braided line: Braided line has surged in popularity in recent years, known for its strength, sensitivity, and low stretch. It's excellent for deep-water fishing and detecting subtle bites, but its lack of stretch can lead to pulled hooks if not handled carefully. While more expensive than monofilament, its durability and casting distance make it a favorite among many anglers (McNally, 2018).

Fluorocarbon line: Fluorocarbon line offers excellent invisibility underwater, making it ideal for clear water fishing. It sinks faster than mono and has less stretch, providing better sensitivity and hook-setting power. Though it can be stiffer and trickier to tie knots, its abrasion resistance and low visibility make it a top choice for many anglers (McNally, 2018).

Each type of fishing line has its strengths and weaknesses, so consider your fishing style and preferences when making your selection. Whether you're casting for bass in a local pond or trolling for marlin in the open ocean, choosing the right fishing line can make all the difference in your angling adventures.

Hooks, Baits, and Lures

Alright, folks, let's talk hooks, baits, and lures—the bread and butter of any angler's tackle box!

Hooks

Choosing the right hook might seem as simple as picking a size from a chart, but trust me, it's a bit more intricate than that. Hooks come in various sizes and types, each serving its unique purpose in helping you land that prized catch.

First off, let's decipher hook sizes. They range from tiny size 30 to hefty 27/0, catering to fish of all shapes and sizes. And don't get me started on the "aughts"—those numbers on the right side that make things even more interesting. It's like hook-size algebra, but once you get the hang of it, you'll be hooking 'em like a pro.

Now, onto the types of hooks you need in your tackle box (Albert, 2019):

- **Bait holder hooks:** These babies keep your bait secure with barbs on the shank, ensuring it stays put until a fish decides to take a nibble. Just beware of their barbs—they can cause a bit of damage, so they're not ideal for catch-and-release scenarios.

- **Worm hooks:** If you're into worm fishing, you and worm hooks are practically besties. Their unique bend near the eye keeps your plastic worm in place while waiting for that unsuspecting fish to take the bait.

- **Jig hooks:** Simple yet effective, jig hooks are designed to maximize lure movement in the water. Plus, they're easy to adapt for catch-and-release by tweaking the barb on the point.

- **Circle hooks:** Talk about fish-friendly! Circle hooks are designed to hook fish in the corner of the mouth, reducing the risk of deep hooking and making catch-and-release a breeze. Just remember to let them set firmly before applying pressure.

- **Weedless hooks:** Perfect for bass anglers navigating through heavy vegetation, these hooks feature a thin guard to prevent snagging every plant in the pond. They strike a balance between keeping your bait secure and avoiding a messy retrieval.

- **Treble hooks:** When you need triple the chance of a hookup, treble hooks come to the rescue. With three points, they offer increased odds of catching your target, but be cautious—they can be tricky to remove without a few extra precautions.

Now, a little more about circle hooks in particular. Circle hooks, with their ingenious design, prioritize the welfare of the fish. By targeting the corner of the mouth, they minimize injury and facilitate easier release. Their versatility extends to various bait types, accommodating both live and dead offerings for a wide range of species. Anglers employ a finesse technique, relying on a "dead stick" approach, where gentle pressure sets the hook without risking excessive force. Notably, circle hooks have been instrumental in reducing deep hooking instances, contrasting with the more hazardous tendencies of J-hooks. Studies affirm their efficacy, particularly in enhancing the survival rates of species like striped bass during catch and release (CIRCLE HOOKS, n.d.).

And the list goes on! From Siwash hooks to Kahle hooks, each type serves a specific purpose in your fishing arsenal. So, next time you're stocking up on gear, remember that the right hook can make all the difference between a successful fishing trip and one that got away.

Baits

Alright, let's dive into the age-old debate about live bait versus artificial bait. Each has its loyal fanbase, but which one should you choose? Let's weigh the pros and cons.

First up, live bait. Worms and minnows are classics in the angler's arsenal. They offer an irresistible allure to many fish species. There's something about the wriggling motion of a live worm or the shimmer of a lively minnow that drives fish wild. Plus, live bait can be versatile and suitable for various fishing conditions and species.

However, live bait does come with its challenges. For one, it requires maintenance. You've got to keep those worms or minnows alive and kicking, which means carrying bait containers, aerators, and maybe even a portable cooler. Not to mention, live bait can be messy, with worms squirming and minnows flopping around.

Now, let's talk about artificial bait. Plastic worms, soft plastics, and other artificial lures have their own set of perks. They're durable, reusable, and come in a vast array of colors, shapes, and sizes. This variety allows you to experiment and find the perfect lure to match the fish's preferences and the fishing conditions.

Artificial bait also offers convenience. You don't have to worry about keeping them alive or dealing with messy bait containers. Just toss them in your tackle box, and you're good to go whenever inspiration strikes.

However, artificial bait requires a bit more skill to use effectively. You've got to master techniques like jigging, flipping, and pitching to mimic natural prey and entice fish to strike. Plus, there's the learning curve of figuring out which lure works best in different situations.

So, which one is better? Well, it depends on various factors, including the fish species you're targeting, the fishing environment, and personal preference. Some anglers swear by live bait for its authenticity and effectiveness, while others prefer the versatility and convenience of artificial bait.

Ultimately, the best approach is to experiment with both live and artificial baits and see what works best for you. Mix it up, try different techniques, and don't be afraid to switch things up if one method isn't producing results.

Tips for Bait Selection

Let me share some tips to help you pick the perfect bait for your next fishing adventure.

- Consider the type of fish you're targeting. Different fish have different preferences when it comes to food, so you'll want to tailor your bait choice accordingly. Do a bit of research to find out what your target fish like to eat and choose bait that matches their natural diet. For example, if you're going after bass, they're big fans of live bait like worms or minnows. But if you're targeting trout, they might go crazy for a shiny spinner or a colorful fly.

- Next, think about the water conditions. Is it clear or murky? Is the water shallow or deep? These factors can all affect which bait will be most effective. In clear water, fish might be more wary of large, obvious baits, so you might want to opt for something more subtle and natural-looking. On the other hand, in murky water, fish rely more on their sense of smell and vibration to find food, so a stinkier bait or a noisy lure might be the way to go.

- Another thing to consider is the time of year. Fish behavior can change with the seasons, so what works in the summer might not be as effective in the winter. For example, in the spring, fish might be more active and willing to chase down fast-moving lures, while in the fall, they might be more focused on feeding before winter sets in. Pay attention to seasonal patterns and adjust your bait selection accordingly.

- Now, let's talk about live bait versus artificial bait. Live bait can be incredibly effective because it's what fish are used to eating in their natural environment. Plus, it's constantly moving and wriggling, which can attract the attention of nearby fish. On the other hand, artificial bait can be more convenient and versatile. You don't have to worry about keeping it alive or fresh, and you can experiment with different colors, sizes, and styles to see what works best.

- When in doubt, don't be afraid to ask for advice. Whether it's from fellow anglers, bait and tackle shops, or online forums, there's a wealth of knowledge out there just waiting to be tapped into. People love to share their tips and tricks, so don't hesitate to reach out and get some guidance if you're feeling unsure.

- And finally, don't be afraid to experiment. Fishing is as much an art as it is a science, and sometimes the best way to figure out what works is to try different things and see what happens. Don't be afraid to mix it up and think outside the box. Who knows, you might just stumble upon the perfect bait that nobody else has thought of yet!

Lures

When it comes to fishing, selecting the right lure can make all the difference between reeling in a trophy catch and going home empty-handed. So, let's break down a few popular types: spinnerbaits, crankbaits, and jigs.

First up, spinnerbaits. These flashy lures are like the rock stars of the fishing world, attracting attention with their spinning blades and vibrant skirts. Spinnerbaits are fantastic for covering a lot of water quickly, making them ideal for targeting active fish in open water or around structures like docks and weed beds. They're versatile too, working well in both shallow and deep water.

Next, crankbaits. These lures are the go-getters of the fishing scene, diving down deep to where the fish lurk and enticing strikes with their lifelike swimming action. Crankbaits come in various shapes, sizes, and diving depths, allowing you to match the lure to the water conditions and the fish's preferences. They're perfect for targeting predatory fish like bass, pike, and walleye.

And last but not least, jigs. These lures are the workhorses of the fishing world, offering versatility and effectiveness in a compact package. Jigs consist of a weighted head and a trailing skirt or soft plastic bait, making them perfect for bouncing along the bottom or flipping into cover. They're incredibly versatile, allowing you to fish them in various ways, from dragging them slowly along the bottom to hopping them erratically through the water column.

Now, how do you choose the right lure for your fishing adventure? Well, it all boils down to understanding your target fish and the water conditions. If you're going after aggressive predators in murky water, a spinnerbait might be your best bet for drawing strikes with its flashy presentation. On the other hand, if you're targeting bottom-dwelling fish in clear water, a jig might be more effective for enticing bites with its subtle action.

Similarly, crankbaits excel in situations where you need to cover a lot of water quickly and reach specific depths where the fish are holding. They come in shallow-running, medium-diving, and deep-diving models, allowing you to adjust your presentation based on the water depth and the fish's behavior.

Ultimately, the key to selecting the right lure is to experiment and adapt to the conditions. Pay attention to the fish's behavior, the water temperature, and the presence of structure or baitfish. By matching your lure choice to the prevailing conditions, you'll increase your chances of success and enjoy a more rewarding fishing experience.

Knot Tying

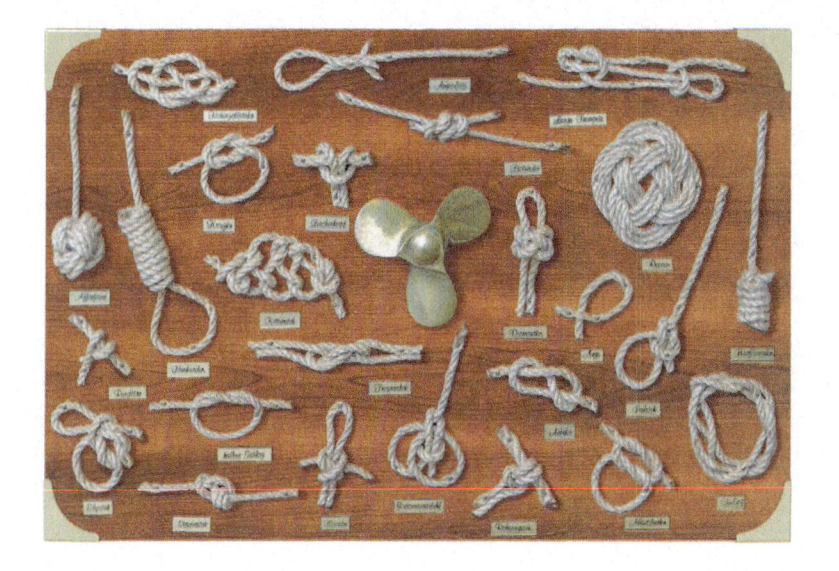

Alright, let's dive into some basic fishing knots that every angler should have in their repertoire. First up, we've got the improved clinch knot. This trusty knot is like the Swiss Army knife of fishing knots—it's versatile, reliable, and easy to tie.

To tie the improved clinch knot, start by passing about five to seven inches of line through the eye of your tackle. Then, wrap that end around the line above the eye about five to seven times, depending on the weight of your line. Hold those wraps in place above the eye, making sure they don't unravel, and then pass the loose end of the line through the loop closest to the eye. Finally, pass the loose end through the loop you just created behind the eye, and pull the knot snug. Trim any excess line, wet the knot if you like for extra tightening, and you're good to go!

Next up, we've got the Palomar knot. This knot is a breeze to tie and is perfect for braided lines, although it's not ideal for most monofilament lines.

To tie the Palomar knot, start by pulling a generous amount of line through the eye of your tackle. Then, pass the loose end back through to create a large loop. With one hand, hold the loose end and the line leading to your reel between your fingers. With your other hand, make a simple overhand knot with the loop, but don't tighten it just yet. Pass your tackle—whether it's a hook, sinker, or swivel—through the loop, snug the knot, trim off any excess line, and you're ready to hit the water!

Last but not least, let's talk about the loop knot. This knot is perfect for giving your lures maximum freedom of movement in the water, making it a favorite among anglers targeting species like crappie.

To tie the loop knot, start by passing your line through the eye of your lure. Then, double back the tag end a few times to create a loop around your hand or fingers. Twist that loop to create a hoop, and then pass the lure through the hoop you've created. Work the knot down toward the eye of the lure, cinching the tag end and the main line independently until the knot is snug. Finally, trim any excess line, and you're all set!

With a bit of practice, you'll be tying these knots like a pro in no time. Whether you're a beginner angler or a seasoned veteran, having these basic fishing knots in your arsenal will help ensure that you're always ready for whatever the fish throw your way.

Casting Techniques

It's time we discuss casting techniques—a crucial skill for any angler looking to land the big one. We'll cover three fundamental casting techniques: overhead casting, sidearm casting, and pitching. Plus, we'll dive into some tips for improving both accuracy and distance in your casts.

First up, we've got overhead casting, perhaps the most common casting technique used by anglers worldwide. To execute an overhead cast, start by holding your rod with both hands, one hand gripping the rod's handle and the other hand positioned further up the rod's shaft. Next, with a smooth and controlled motion, bring the rod back behind your shoulder and then forward in a fluid motion, releasing the line as you bring the rod forward. The key here is to use your wrist and forearm to generate power while maintaining control over the direction of your cast. Practice this motion until it becomes second nature, and you'll be casting like a pro in no time.

Next, let's talk about sidearm casting—a technique that's particularly useful when fishing in tight spaces or under low-hanging vegetation. To execute a sidearm cast, hold your rod parallel to the water's surface, with your casting hand positioned to the side of your body. Then, using a smooth and controlled motion, sweep the rod forward and slightly upward, releasing the line as you do so. The goal here is to keep your cast low to the water's surface, allowing you to slip your bait or lure into tight spots with ease. With a bit of practice, you'll be sidearm casting like a champ.

Last but not least, let's discuss pitching—a casting technique that's perfect for dropping your bait or lure with pinpoint accuracy. To execute a pitch cast, start by holding your rod with one hand and gripping it near the reel seat. Then, using your wrist and forearm, flick the rod forward in a short, controlled motion, releasing the line as you do so. The goal here is to deliver your bait or lure with precision, dropping it softly into the water without creating a big splash. Practice pitching to different targets, adjusting the force and angle of your cast as needed to hone your accuracy.

Now, let's talk about how to improve both the accuracy and distance of your casts. First, focus on your casting mechanics—make sure you're using smooth, fluid motions and you're applying the right amount of power to your cast. Practice regularly to develop muscle memory and fine-tune your technique.

Next, pay attention to your rod and reel setup. Make sure your rod is matched to the type of fishing you're doing and that your reel is properly spooled with line. Experiment with different rod actions and reel speeds to find what works best for you.

Additionally, consider the weight and aerodynamics of your bait or lure. Lighter baits will require adjustments to your casting technique, while more aerodynamic lures will travel farther with less effort.

Finally, don't underestimate the importance of practice. The more time you spend casting, the better you'll become. Experiment with different casting techniques, try casting from different angles and positions, and challenge yourself to cast accurately at various distances. With dedication and perseverance, you'll soon find yourself casting with precision and confidence every time you hit the water.

Hook Setting

Picture this: You're out on the water, rod in hand, and suddenly you feel a tug on the line. That's your cue to spring into action. When a fish strikes, you want to snap that rod up over your shoulder or to the side, kind of like you're casting a spell with your fishing rod. But before you do that, reel in any slack line and point your rod toward the fish. These two steps are crucial for a successful hookset. Without them, you might miss your chance to reel in the big one.

Now, as you reel in and move your rod toward the fish, you'll start to feel its weight. Once that slack is gone and you feel that tug, it's time to strike. Keep your elbows in and with a quick flick of your wrist, snap that rod up and over your shoulder. It's like setting off a fishing fireworks show!

But we're not done yet, folks. Immediately after setting the hook, you've gotta keep that pressure on the fish. Crank that reel a few times to really drive those hooks home, especially if you're fishing in thick vegetation or going after toothy critters. Sometimes, the initial snap of the rod isn't enough to bury those hooks deep, so a few extra cranks of the reel can seal the deal.

Now, how hard you set that hook and how fast you do it depends on a few things. Different fish require different approaches. Soft-mouthed fish like crappie or light biters like certain trout only need a gentle, sweeping hookset. You don't wanna go yanking the hook out of their mouths! But if you're going after hard-mouthed pike or aggressive fish, you'll need to put some muscle into it. And if you really need that extra oomph, take a step back for more leverage and power.

Alright, let's talk about five golden rules of hook-setting that'll help you reel in those beauties:

1. **Rule one:** Feel the weight of the fish before setting the hook. Don't get too trigger-happy, especially with topwater fishing. Wait till you feel that weight, then let 'em have it!

2. **Rule two:** Timing is everything. If those fish are hitting hard and fast, set that hook quickly. But if they're just nibbling, give 'em a little more time to take the bait before you strike.

3. **Rule three:** No slack allowed. Keep that line tight at all times, folks. It's the key to feeling those strikes and delivering a killer hookset.

4. **Rule four:** Don't dilly-dally with live bait. Those fish won't wait forever to chow down. Set that hook sooner rather than later to avoid gut-hooking those suckers.

5. **Rule five:** Trolling? The jury's still out on whether you need to set the hook while trolling. If you're zooming along with a tight drag, the momentum of the boat might do the trick. But if you're trolling slowly with a loose drag, go ahead and set that hook.

Remember, timing is everything, and when in doubt, set that hook!

Fishing Locations

Researching and identifying suitable fishing spots can make all the difference between a successful day on the water and coming home empty-handed. Here's how to do it like a pro.

First things first, do your homework. Thanks to the wonders of modern technology, there are plenty of resources available to help you research potential fishing spots. Start by checking online forums, fishing websites, and social media groups dedicated to your local area. These platforms are often filled with valuable insights and firsthand experiences from fellow anglers who know the waters like the back of their hand.

Next, consider factors like water temperature, depth, and structure. Fish are creatures of habit, and they tend to gravitate toward areas that offer the ideal conditions for feeding and shelter. Pay attention to water temperature trends—fish are more active in warmer water, so target areas where the temperature is on the rise. Similarly, look for areas with varying depths and underwater structures like rocks, submerged trees, and drop-offs. These features provide cover for fish and create natural feeding opportunities.

When scouting potential fishing spots, keep an eye out for signs of life. Look for fish jumping out of the water, birds diving for food, or even ripples on the surface that indicate the presence of feeding fish below. These visual cues can help you pinpoint active fishing areas and increase your chances of success.

Another important factor to consider is access. Even the best fishing spot in the world won't do you much good if you can't reach it. Look for locations that are easily accessible by foot, boat, or kayak, depending on your preferred method of fishing. Consider factors like parking availability, proximity to boat ramps or launch sites, and any potential obstacles or hazards you may encounter along the way.

Once you've narrowed down your list of potential fishing spots, it's time to put your research to the test. Get out on the water and explore each location firsthand, taking note of water conditions, fish activity, and any other relevant observations. Keep a log of your findings, including details like water temperature, weather conditions, and bait/lure preferences. This information will become invaluable as you continue to refine your fishing strategy over time.

Remember, finding the perfect fishing spot is as much about trial and error as it is about research and preparation. Don't be afraid to experiment with different locations, techniques, and baits/lures until you find what works best for you. And above all, enjoy the process—fishing is as much about the journey as it is about the destination. So, get out there, explore new waters, and reel in some memories that will last a lifetime!

Patience

The moment you saw this heading, I know what you're thinking: *Patience? Isn't that just a fancy word for sitting around and doing nothing?* Well, not quite! Patience is more than just waiting for a fish to bite—it's about embracing the tranquility of the water, enjoying the beauty of nature, and savoring the anticipation of that epic battle between angler and fish.

First things first, let's address the elephant in the room: waiting for bites. Yes, it's true that fishing involves a fair amount of downtime, but that's all part of the fun! Instead of staring at your fishing rod like it's a ticking time bomb, take this opportunity to relax and unwind. Crack open a cold beverage, soak up some sunshine, and let the rhythm of the water soothe your soul. Who knows, you might even catch a nap along with your next big catch!

Now, when it comes to waiting for those elusive bites, patience is key. Fish aren't exactly known for their punctuality, so be prepared to wait it out. But here's the thing: Fishing isn't just about catching fish—it's about the thrill of the chase, the excitement of the unknown, and the satisfaction of finally reeling in that big one. So, take a deep breath, cast your line, and trust that good things come to those who wait.

While you're biding your time, why not take the opportunity to observe the water? Fish are sneaky little creatures, and they often give themselves away with subtle clues like ripples on the surface, underwater movement, or the occasional splash. Keep an eye out for these telltale signs, and you'll be one step closer to hooking your next trophy fish.

Of course, patience isn't just about waiting—it's also about staying focused and attentive. Keep your senses sharp, your reflexes primed, and your fishing rod at the ready. You never know when that big bite will come, so be prepared to spring into action at a moment's notice. And remember, fishing is a game of patience and perseverance, so don't let a few missed bites dampen your spirits. Keep casting, keep reeling, and keep that smile on your face—you're one step closer to landing the catch of a lifetime!

Now, let's talk about tips for staying patient while you're out on the water.

- First and foremost, bring along some snacks! There's nothing like a tasty treat to help pass the time while you're waiting for that next big bite. Plus, a full belly makes for a happy angler, so stock up on your favorite snacks and enjoy a mini picnic by the water's edge.
- Next, why not try some mindfulness techniques to help calm your mind and soothe your soul? Take a moment to focus on your breath, listen to the sounds of nature, and appreciate the beauty of your surroundings. Fishing is as much about the experience as it is about the catch, so take this opportunity to connect with the great outdoors and recharge your batteries.
- And finally, don't forget to bring along some entertainment to help pass the time. Whether it's a good book, your favorite podcast, or a lively conversation with your fishing buddies, having something to occupy your mind can make those long hours on the water fly by in a flash.

Fish Handling and Safety

Knowing the art of fish handling and safety is crucial because nothing ruins a good fishing trip like mishandling your catch. Whether you're practicing catch-and-release or planning to cook up a storm later, it's essential to treat your finned friends with care and respect.

Fish Handling

First up, let's talk about proper catch-and-release techniques. Now, I know it's tempting to keep every fish you catch, but sometimes it's best to let them go and live to fight another day. When you're out on the water, make sure to stay close to your rod or line—no wandering off for a snack break! Being nearby reduces the risk of fish swallowing hooks deeply, which can cause serious harm.

And when it comes to landing your catch, speed is key. A tired fish is more susceptible to injury and stress, so try to reel it in as quickly as possible. Using a landing net can also help minimize handling time and stress, especially for those big, feisty fish that like to put up a fight.

Now, onto the nitty-gritty of handling your catch. Once you've landed your fish, keep it wet and calm to avoid unnecessary stress and injury. Support the fish properly—never hold it by the gills—and handle it gently with wet hands or gloves to protect its delicate mucus layer.

When it's time to remove the hook, work quickly and calmly. Use the right tools—a good pair of needle-nosed pliers or hook removers can make the job much easier. If the hook is deeply embedded or difficult to remove, don't force it. Sometimes it's best to cut the line and let the fish go with the hook still in place.

Now, onto the all-important moment of releasing your fish back into the wild. Before you let it go, make sure it's fully recovered and ready to swim away on its own. Hold the fish underwater, in an upright position, and wait until you see its gills opening and closing before releasing it. If the fish seems to be struggling, consider moving it to calmer water to give it a better chance of survival.

And let's not forget about minimizing stress on the fish throughout the handling process. Use appropriate gear to minimize fight time, avoid stainless steel hooks that can cause unnecessary damage, and opt for circle hooks to increase the chances of mouth hooking. Remember, the goal is to minimize handling and air exposure to give your catch the best chance of making it back to the water safely.

Safety

No fishing trip is worth risking life and limb for. Whether you're out on the open water or casting a line from the shore, it's crucial to stay aware of your surroundings and come prepared with the right gear.

Always be mindful of your surroundings. Look out for any potential hazards like slippery rocks, strong currents, or low-hanging branches. And if you're fishing from a boat, make sure everyone on board is wearing a life jacket. It might not be the most fashionable accessory, but it could save your life in an emergency.

Now, let's talk clothing. When you're spending hours out in the sun, it's important to dress appropriately to protect yourself from harmful UV rays. Wear lightweight, breathable clothing that covers your skin, along with a wide-brimmed hat to shield your face and neck from the sun. And don't forget the sunscreen! Slather on a generous amount of SPF to prevent painful sunburns and reduce the risk of skin cancer.

Oh, and speaking of pests, don't let those pesky bugs ruin your fishing fun. Bring along some insect repellent to keep mosquitoes and other critters at bay. Trust me, nothing puts a damper on a fishing trip like getting eaten alive by bugs.

Now, let's talk about essential safety gear. In addition to sunscreen, a hat, and insect repellent, there are a few other items you should never leave home without. First aid kit? Check. You never know when you might need a bandage or some antiseptic cream for those inevitable cuts and scrapes. And don't forget a reliable flashlight or headlamp in case you find yourself out after dark. It's always better to be safe than sorry, especially when you're miles away from civilization.

And last but not least, always let someone know where you're going and when you expect to be back. It might sound like common sense, but you'd be surprised how many anglers head out on the water without telling anyone their plans. If something were to go wrong, you want someone to know where to look for you.

Remember, the goal is to have fun and reel in some big catches, but not at the expense of your safety.

Weather Awareness and Environmental Respect

Weather awareness and environmental respect are key to being a responsible angler, so let's dive in.

First off, let's chat about keeping an eye on the weather. You might be thinking, *What does the weather have to do with fishing?* Well, my friend, a lot more than you might think. Fish are creatures of habit, and they're greatly influenced by weather conditions. So, before you head out on your fishing excursion, take a moment to check the forecast. Rain, wind, temperature changes—they all play a role in fish behavior. For example, some fish are more active when it's overcast, while others prefer sunny days. By monitoring the weather, you can better predict where the fish might be hanging out and adjust your strategy accordingly.

Now, let's talk about ethical angling principles and conservation guidelines. As anglers, it's our responsibility to respect the environment and the fish that call it home. That means following catch limits, practicing catch and release when appropriate, and using sustainable fishing practices. Take only what you need, and release the rest to ensure healthy fish populations for future generations. And while you're at it, why not lend a hand in conservation efforts? Get involved with local fishing clubs or environmental organizations that work to protect our waterways and promote responsible angling practices. Every little bit helps!

And let's not forget about leaving no trace. Just like the old saying goes, "Take only pictures, leave only footprints." When you're out enjoying nature, be sure to clean up after yourself and leave your fishing spot better than you found it. Pack out all your trash, including fishing line, bait containers, and any other litter you may have accumulated. And if you see someone else's trash lying around, do the planet a solid and pick it up. Together, we can keep our waterways clean and pristine for everyone to enjoy.

By staying aware of the weather, respecting the environment, and practicing ethical angling, we can all do our part to ensure that fishing remains a fun and sustainable activity for generations to come. So, get out there, cast a line, and remember to leave nothing behind but good memories.

Weather Interpretation

Paying attention to the forecast and understanding how weather patterns affect fish behavior is important. Let's break down the basics of weather interpretation. Keep an eye on the sky and look for clues like cloud cover, wind direction, and air pressure. These factors can give you valuable insight into what the weather has in store.

- Cloud cover is a big one. On sunny days, fish tend to seek shelter in deeper waters or under cover to avoid the bright sunlight. But when clouds roll in, they feel more comfortable venturing out into the open to feed. Overcast skies can also lead to better fishing conditions as they diffuse the light and reduce glare on the water, making it easier for fish to spot your bait.

- Next up, wind direction. Fish are sensitive to changes in wind direction as it affects the distribution of food sources in the water. Onshore winds, blowing from the water toward the shore, can push baitfish closer to the shoreline, attracting predators like bass and trout. Offshore winds, blowing from the shore out to sea, can concentrate baitfish in deeper waters, drawing in larger predators like walleye and pike.

- Now let's talk about air pressure. Changes in air pressure, indicated by the rise and fall of a barometer, can have a significant impact on fish behavior. When air pressure is high and rising, fish tend to become more active and feed more aggressively. Conversely, when air pressure is low and falling, fish may become lethargic and less inclined to bite. Keep an eye on the barometer and plan your fishing trips accordingly.

- Temperature plays a big role, too. Fish are cold-blooded creatures, which means their metabolism and activity levels are directly influenced by water temperature. In general, warmer water temperatures lead to increased fish activity and feeding behavior, while colder water temperatures can slow them down. Pay attention to seasonal temperature trends and adjust your fishing strategies accordingly.

- Rain is another important factor to consider. A light drizzle or rain shower can actually improve fishing conditions by washing insects and other food sources into the water, enticing fish to feed. However, heavy rain can muddy the water and make it difficult for fish to see your bait. If it's raining cats and dogs, you might want to consider calling it a day and waiting for clearer skies.

- Thunderstorms are a whole different ball game. Not only are they dangerous to be out on the water in, but they can also send fish into hiding. Lightning can spook fish and cause them to retreat to deeper waters or seek shelter under cover. If you hear thunder or see lightning in the distance, it's time to pack up and head for shore.

Remember, fishing is all about adapting to the conditions and making the most of what nature throws your way.

Fish Identification Tips

Identifying fish can be a bit like solving a puzzle—challenging but oh-so-rewarding when you get it right. So, let's dive into some tips to help you become a fish identification master.

- First off, know your area. Before you hit the water, do some research on the fish species expected in the waters you'll be exploring. Having a list of potential candidates narrows down the possibilities, making it easier to identify what you catch. If you stumble upon a species not known in the area, it might be time to reconsider your ID or seek confirmation.

- Now, let's talk resources. A good regional guidebook is your best friend. But don't underestimate the power of online databases, even though they might lack quality control. Be cautious of misidentifications—like listing slimy sculpin in BC coastal streams where they don't belong. Sometimes folks just like the name and jump to conclusions!

- Know your endangered and invasive species. Getting these wrong can have serious consequences. If you suspect you've found one, document it carefully or even collect it as a voucher specimen for further analysis.

- Consider habitat. Different fish species have different hangouts. Whether it's a deep pool or a riffle, headwaters, or lower reaches, these habitat clues can help narrow down your options.

- Now, let's talk about looks. Forget about color—it's too variable. Instead, focus on morphological features like fin count, mouth size, or lateral line pattern. These characteristics don't change based on water clarity or time of year.

- Never guess. If you're not sure, admit it. It's better to say you caught a Lamprey than misidentify it. Trust me, I've heard horror stories of misidentifications leading to wasted time and credibility damage.

- Want to level up your ID skills? Create your own ID key. Start with a smaller group, like sculpins or basses, and work your way up. This hands-on approach will boost your confidence and understanding like nothing else.

- When in doubt, snap some pics and consult with experts. Photograph the fish from different angles, include something for scale, and reach out to knowledgeable colleagues. Sometimes, the most honest thing you can say is "I don't know."

- If identification is crucial and it's not an endangered species, consider collecting a voucher specimen. These are individuals preserved for ID and long-term archiving, ensuring accurate identification.

Fish identification isn't just about knowing species in the field—it's also about knowing what to do when you're stumped. These tips will help you navigate the murky waters of fish ID and become a pro in no time.

Watercraft Navigation

Alright, let's talk about navigating the waters like a pro. Whether you're in a kayak, canoe, or a full-fledged fishing boat, knowing how to maneuver on the water is key to a successful fishing trip. Here are some tips to help you navigate like a seasoned sailor.

- First things first, know your watercraft. Whether it's your own or a rental, familiarize yourself with its features and controls. Practice paddling or steering in calm waters before heading out into more challenging conditions.

- Safety first, folks. Always wear your life jacket, no matter how confident a swimmer you are. It's like wearing a seatbelt—you hope you won't need it, but it's there just in case.

- Now, let's talk about planning your route. Before you set sail, check the weather forecast and tide tables. You don't want to get caught in rough waters or strong currents unexpectedly. Plot your course, taking into account any obstacles like rocks, shoals, or shallow areas.

- Keep an eye on your surroundings as you navigate. Look out for other boats, kayakers, or swimmers, and always yield to larger vessels. Remember, you're not the only one out there.

- When paddling, use proper techniques to conserve energy and maintain control. Keep your strokes smooth and even, and use your torso to power your paddle rather than just your arms. And don't forget to switch sides regularly to avoid muscle fatigue.

- If you're in a motorized boat, follow the rules of the waterway. Stay to the right, obey speed limits, and yield to nonmotorized craft. And please, for the love of fishing, don't drink and boat. Save the celebratory beverages for when you're safely back on shore.

- Navigating in low visibility? Slow down, use your navigation lights, and sound your horn or whistle if necessary. Keep a lookout for buoys, markers, or landmarks to help guide your way.

- When anchoring, choose a spot with good holding ground and enough swinging room. Drop your anchor slowly, letting out enough line to reach the bottom, and secure it firmly. And always double-check that it's holding before you relax and cast your line.

- Now, let's talk about currents and tides. If you're fishing in tidal waters, pay attention to the direction and strength of the current. Fish tend to gather where currents meet, creating prime fishing spots. And remember, the best time to fish is often during the changing tide when baitfish are on the move.

- Lastly, respect the environment. Avoid disturbing wildlife or sensitive habitats, and always pack out what you pack in. Leave no trace, so future generations can enjoy the same pristine waters you did.

Night Fishing

Fishing under the cover of darkness can be an exhilarating experience, but it requires a different approach and some extra precautions to ensure a successful outing. Here are some tips to help you make the most of your night fishing adventures:

- **Choose the right location.** Not all fishing spots are created equal when it comes to night fishing. Look for areas with easy access and minimal obstructions, as navigating in the dark can be challenging. Shallow areas near shorelines, docks, or underwater structures are often productive spots for night fishing, as fish tend to move closer to the shallows under the cover of darkness.

- **Use the right gear.** Night fishing requires some specialized gear to enhance your experience and increase your chances of success. Invest in a quality fishing rod with a sensitive tip and a sturdy reel with a smooth drag system. Consider using braided fishing line, which is highly visible in low light conditions and offers excellent sensitivity for detecting bites.

- **Choose the right bait.** Just like during the day, choosing the right bait is crucial for night fishing success. Many fish species are more active at night and may be more receptive to certain types of bait. Live bait such as minnows, worms, or nightcrawlers can be particularly effective for night fishing, as their natural movement and scent can attract fish in the dark.

- **Embrace the darkness.** Fishing in the dark requires a different mindset than fishing during the day. Embrace the darkness and let your other senses take over. Listen for the sounds of fish breaking the surface or feeding nearby, and pay attention to any subtle movements or vibrations in your line that could indicate a bite.

- **Use light strategically.** While it may seem counterintuitive, excessive light can actually spook fish and make them less likely to bite. Keep your artificial lighting to a minimum and use it strategically to illuminate your immediate fishing area without casting too much light on the water. Red or green light is less likely to disturb fish than white light, so consider using colored light for night fishing.

- **Stay quiet and stealthy.** Fish have keen senses, even in the dark, so it's essential to minimize noise and movement to avoid spooking them. Move quietly and avoid casting with too much force, as the sound of a lure hitting the water can scare off nearby fish. Keep your movements slow and deliberate, and be patient as you wait for the fish to come to you.

- **Be patient:** Patience is key when night fishing. Fish may be less active or more selective in their feeding habits at night, so be prepared to wait for the right opportunity. Don't be discouraged if you don't get immediate results—sometimes, the best bites come when you least expect them.

- **Stay comfortable.** Night fishing can be chilly, especially during the cooler months, so make sure you dress appropriately for the weather. Wear layers to stay warm and dry, and consider bringing along a thermos of hot coffee or cocoa to keep you comfortable during those long nights on the water.

So, there you have it—some tips to help you make the most of your night fishing adventures.

Safety Measures

Whether you're on a boat, by the shore, or out on the ice, there are some key safety measures you should always keep in mind to ensure a safe and enjoyable experience.

- First things first, if you're using a boat, your number one priority should be wearing a life jacket. And don't just wear one yourself—make sure everyone onboard has one too. It's the simplest and most effective way to stay safe on the water, whether you're reeling in the big one or just enjoying the scenery.
- Now, let's talk about inspecting your surroundings. The natural environment can change in the blink of an eye, so it's essential to inspect waterfronts daily. Keep an eye out for any hazards or changes in conditions that could affect your safety.
- Another crucial point: respect the rules and regulations of the area you're fishing in. If an area is declared off-limits, there's probably a good reason for it—whether it's to protect wildlife, vegetation, or your own safety. Always fish in permitted areas to avoid any unnecessary risks.
- And speaking of risks, different environments call for different safety measures. If you're out on the ice, for example, avoid old ice—it's just not worth the risk. Always be aware of the specific hazards and safety tips relevant to your fishing environment.
- Now, let's talk about being prepared. Bring along extra safety items like water, flashlights, maps, and a cell phone or radio. You never know when you might need them, so it's better to be safe than sorry.
- And don't forget about footwear. Always wear appropriate footwear for the conditions you'll be fishing in. Whether it's sturdy boots for hiking to your favorite spot or water shoes for wading in the shallows, having the right footwear can make all

the difference.

- Now, let's talk about staying comfortable and protected from the elements. Wear waterproof sunscreen with an SPF of at least 15 to protect yourself from the sun's harmful rays. Layer up with thin clothing that can be easily adjusted to keep you warm and dry, and don't forget about protection from insects—proper clothing and repellents are a must.

- When it comes to handling equipment, keep your fishing knives sharp and always cover the blade when not in use. And when handling fish, use caution when baiting and removing hooks to avoid any accidents or injuries.

Fish Cleaning and Filleting

Even though this topic will be covered in greater detail in Chapter 4, let's talk about it briefly. Here's a quick rundown to get you started:

1. Before you begin, make sure you have all the necessary tools on hand. You'll need a sharp fillet knife, a cutting board, and a clean surface to work on. Having a pair of kitchen shears can also be handy for removing fins and other small parts.

2. For the best results, clean and fillet your fish as soon as possible after catching it. Fresh fish are easier to work with and yield better-tasting fillets.

3. If your fish still has scales, you'll need to remove them before filleting. Use a fish scaler or the back of your knife to scrape against the grain of the scales until they're all removed.

4. Lay your fish flat on the cutting board and make a shallow incision behind the gills, running down to the belly. Be careful not to cut too deep—you just want to pierce the skin to create an entry point for your fillet knife.

5. Insert your fillet knife into the incision you made and carefully follow the backbone of the fish, cutting along one

side from head to tail. Use smooth, steady strokes and let the knife do the work.

6. Once you've cut along one side of the backbone, use your knife to separate the fillet from the ribs and belly of the fish. Work slowly and carefully to avoid leaving any meat behind.

7. Flip the fish over and repeat the process on the other side to remove the second fillet. Make sure to clean any remaining bits of flesh and bone from the carcass.

8. If you prefer skinless fillets, you can use your fillet knife to carefully remove the skin from each fillet. Start at the tail end and slide your knife between the flesh and the skin, using a gentle sawing motion to separate them.

9. Once you've filleted your fish, give the fillets a thorough rinse under cold water to remove any remaining scales or debris. Pat them dry with paper towels before cooking or storing them.

10. Finally, make sure to dispose of any fish waste responsibly. You can compost fish scraps or throw them in the trash, but avoid dumping them in bodies of water where they can attract scavengers or contribute to pollution.

Fish Finding Technology

Fish finders are like magic windows that show you what's happening beneath your boat. They use sonar technology to create a graphic representation of the underwater world, helping you spot fish, locate structures, and navigate like a pro.

Now, when it comes to choosing a fish finder, there are a few things to consider:

- **Type of unit:** You've got options! There are standalone fish finders that focus solely on sonar, combination units that include both fish finding and GPS navigation, and fully-networked systems that can do just about everything but cook you dinner.

- **Size and resolution:** Bigger isn't always better, but when it comes to fish finders, a larger display can make it easier to see what's going on below. Look for a unit with a clear, high-resolution display that's easy to read even in bright sunlight.
- **Transmitting power and frequencies:** Depending on where you fish—whether it's inland lakes, coastal waters, or deep offshore spots—you'll need to choose a fish finder with the right transmitting power and frequency range to give you the best results.
- **GPS integration:** If you're the type who likes to know exactly where you are on the water, consider a fish finder with built-in GPS. This can be especially handy for navigating to your favorite fishing spots and marking waypoints for future trips.

Now, let's break down your options (Burden, 2024):

- **Standalone fish finder:** Perfect for anglers who just want to focus on finding fish. These units offer the biggest displays and the most performance for your buck. Great for small boats and budget-conscious fishermen.
- **Combination fish finder/Chartplotter:** Ideal for mid-sized boats, these units offer the best of both worlds—fish finding and GPS navigation—in one convenient package. You can view both functions on a split screen or toggle between them as needed.
- **Fully-networked systems:** For serious anglers with larger vessels, these systems are the ultimate fishing companions. They can do it all—from sonar and GPS to radar, video, and even satellite radio. Plus, you can control them from your smartphone for maximum convenience.

Whether you're casting lines in a cozy cove or venturing into the open ocean, a fish finder can be your secret weapon for finding fish and navigating with confidence. Choose the right unit for your needs, and get ready to reel in the big ones like never before!

Deep Sea Fishing

Here are some tips to help you reel in those big catches and make the most out of your ocean adventures:

- Before you set sail, make sure all your fishing gear is in top-notch condition. Check your rods, reels, and lines for any damage, and don't forget about your safety gear too—life jackets and other safety equipment should be in good working order.
- Pelagic fish like to move around, so it's essential to gather the latest intel before heading out. Talk to fellow anglers, check local tackle shops, and look up current reports online to find out where the fish are biting.
- Keep an eye out for visible structures on the water's surface, like floating debris or color changes, as these can attract fish. Pay attention to any anomalies you see—they could lead you to a hotspot.
- If you're not having luck with your current setup, don't be afraid to change things up. Adjust your trolling speed, switch up your bait presentation, or move to a different spot to increase your chances of success.
- When you get a strike, try to turn it into multiple hook-ups. Keep other lines in the water and be ready to deploy additional bait to capitalize on the action.
- Don't get too hung up on catching a specific species. If you spot fish, go for it—regardless of whether it's your target species or not.
- Fluorocarbon leaders and ball-bearing swivels may cost more, but they can give you a significant advantage when battling deep-sea creatures. Don't skimp on the basics if you want to increase your chances of success.
- Booking a charter can be a great way to learn new techniques and gain valuable knowledge from experienced captains and crew members.

- Use your GPS or chartplotter to mark each bite, so you can quickly return to productive fishing spots in the future.

- If you're serious about deep-sea fishing, consider investing in dredges and teasers to attract more fish to your spread. While they may be challenging to deploy, they can significantly increase your chances of success offshore.

Remember, becoming an expert deep-sea angler takes time and experience, so don't get discouraged if you don't see immediate results.

In conclusion, mastering the basics of fishing is essential for every angler, whether novice or seasoned. From casting techniques to understanding fish behavior, each skill contributes to a successful fishing experience. By practicing patience, safety measures, and environmental awareness, anglers can enjoy the thrill of the catch while respecting nature's delicate balance. Whether you're casting from shore, navigating deep seas, or exploring freshwater streams, the fundamentals discussed in this chapter lay the groundwork for a fulfilling and rewarding journey into the world of fishing. So, grab your gear, embrace the adventure, and let the pursuit of the next big catch begin!

Chapter 2:

Identifying Fish and Where to Find Them

Now that you've got your gear sorted and your tackle box organized, it's time to dive into the fascinating world of fish identification and exploration. Think of this chapter as your underwater GPS, guiding you through the murky depths of rivers, lakes, and oceans to uncover the secrets of the finned creatures that call these waters home.

First things first: Let's talk fish ID. No, not the kind where you're trying to remember if it's a bass or a trout you caught last weekend (although that's important too). We're delving deep into the subtle nuances of each species, from the flashy colors of a rainbow trout to the unmistakable silhouette of a largemouth bass. Trust us, being able to tell your crappie from your catfish will come in handy when bragging about your catch later.

But it's not just about recognizing the fish—it's also about understanding their behavior. Fish are like underwater ninjas, stealthily navigating their way through the water with purpose and precision. I'll teach you how to read their subtle cues, from the way they school to their preferred depths, so you can outsmart them at their own game. After all, there's nothing quite like the satisfaction of outwitting a fish with a brain the size of a pea.

Of course, knowing what kind of fish you're dealing with is only half the battle. You also need to know where to find them. And no, they're not just hanging out at the local fish bar waiting for you to drop by with your fishing rod. Fish have preferences too, whether it's cozying up to submerged structures in a river or lounging in the deep basins of a lake. I'll show you how to uncover these hidden hotspots so you can reel in your next trophy catch with ease.

So, buckle up, anglers, because we're about to set off on a journey into the watery depths where the fish roam free and the adventures are endless. Whether you're a seasoned angler or a newbie just dipping your toes into the world of fishing, there's something here for everyone. Grab your rod, slap on some sunscreen, and let's dive in!

Fish Species Identification

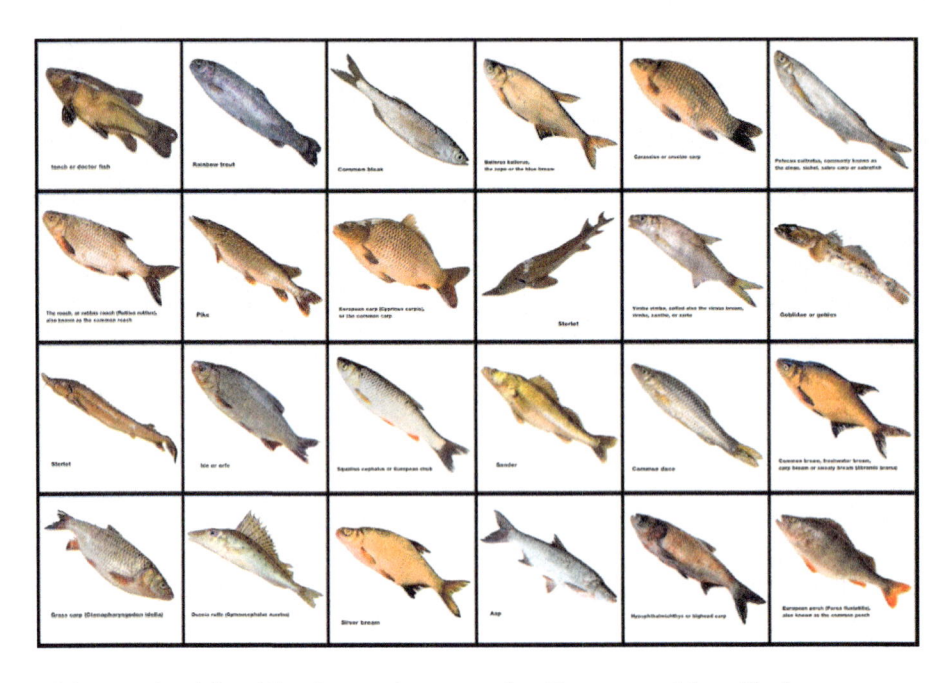

Fish species identification—the art of telling your bluegill from your bullhead, your walleye from your whitefish.

Importance of Recognizing Various Fish Species

You might think, *Why bother? A fish is a fish, right?* Well, my friend, let me tell you why recognizing various fish species is more important than knowing which way the wind is blowing when you're out on the water.

First off, think of it like this: you wouldn't invite just anyone to your backyard barbecue, would you? You'd want to know if you were serving up burgers for the beef lovers or veggie burgers for the herbivores. Similarly, different fish species have different preferences when it comes to bait and habitat. If you want to catch a walleye, you better know how to entice it with the right kind of bait, or you'll end up with an empty net and a growling stomach.

But it's not just about catching fish—it's about understanding the delicate balance of the underwater ecosystem. You see, fish aren't just random creatures swimming around aimlessly; they play specific roles in their environments. Some are top predators, keeping populations of smaller fish in check. Others are bottom feeders, helping to clean up the scraps left behind by their piscine pals. By knowing which fish species are present in a given area, you can get a better sense of the overall health of the ecosystem and how it might be impacted by things like pollution or overfishing.

Plus, let's not forget the bragging rights that come with being able to identify different fish species. There's nothing quite like the feeling of reeling in a whopper of a fish and being able to say, "Yep, that's a northern pike, all right!" It's like being a detective solving a particularly tricky case, only instead of clues, you're following scales and fins.

And let's face it—being able to impress your fishing buddies with your encyclopedic knowledge of fish species is pretty darn cool. Sure, they might roll their eyes and call you a fish nerd behind your back, but secretly they'll be impressed by your expertise. Who knows, they might even start coming to you for advice on how to catch the big ones.

But perhaps the most important reason for recognizing various fish species is conservation. You see, some fish species are more vulnerable to overfishing or habitat destruction than others. By being able to identify these species, anglers can take steps to protect them, whether it's by releasing them back into the water unharmed or advocating for better conservation measures.

So, recognizing various fish species isn't just a fun party trick—it's a vital skill for any angler who wants to reel in the big ones, protect the environment, and earn the respect of their peers.

Distinctive Markings and Characteristics

Alright, let's dive a little deeper into the wonderful world of fish identification. Now, I know what you're thinking—*How on earth am I supposed to tell one fish from another when they all just look like, well, fish?* Fear not, my friend, because I'm here to guide you through the maze of fins, scales, and tails.

First things first, let's talk about those distinctive markings and characteristics that set each fish species apart. It's kind of like playing a game of "spot the difference," only instead of pictures of cats and dogs, you're looking at pictures of bass and bluegill.

Now, some fish have markings that are as plain as the nose on your face—think of the bold stripes of a striped bass or the speckled pattern of a brook trout. These markings are like nature's way of saying, "Hey, look at me, I'm a fish!"

But other fish species are a little sneakier, with markings that blend in perfectly with their surroundings. Take the camouflage patterns of a flounder, for example—one minute, it's there, and the next minute, it's gone, like a fishy magician pulling off the ultimate disappearing act.

Of course, it's not just about the markings—it's also about the little details that make each fish species unique. Pay attention to things like the shape of the mouth, the size of the fins, and the arrangement of the scales. It's these little quirks that can help you differentiate between species, kind of like recognizing your favorite actors by their distinctive features—you know, like Brad Pitt's chiseled jawline or Meryl Streep's expressive eyes.

And let's not forget about size—because as any angler worth their salt knows, size matters. Some fish species are big and beefy, while others are small and sleek. If you reel in a fish that's bigger than your average house cat, chances are you've got yourself a trophy-worthy catch.

But sometimes fish like to play dress-up and change their appearance depending on their mood or surroundings. It's like they're saying, "You can't catch me if you can't see me!" Don't be surprised if that walleye you thought you had figured out suddenly looks like a completely different fish when the light hits it just right.

Ever heard of the red drum? Picture this: You're out on the water, scanning the surface for signs of activity, and suddenly you see a flash of vibrant color beneath the waves. That's your cue to cast your line and reel in one of these beauties. Red drums are named for their distinctive coppery-red coloration, which really pops against the backdrop of murky waters. Plus, they've got those signature black spots near their tails, like little badges of honor.

And then there's the largemouth bass, the holy grail of freshwater fishing. These guys are like the rock stars of the fish world, with their bold horizontal stripes and cavernous mouths that could swallow a small child (okay, maybe not that big, but you get the idea). If you're lucky enough to hook one of these bad boys, hold on tight—because you're in for the fight of your life.

Now, I know what you're thinking—*This all sounds great, but how am I supposed to remember all these details when I'm out on the water?* Well, my friend, that's where practice makes perfect. The more time you spend studying fish species and observing their behavior, the easier it will become to spot those distinctive markings and characteristics.

And hey, if all else fails, there's no shame in busting out your trusty fishing guide and playing a little game of fishy detective. After all, even Sherlock Holmes needed his magnifying glass every now and then.

Examples of Common Fish Species

Alright, let's dive into some examples of common fish species that you're likely to encounter on your fishing adventures.

First up, we've got the striped bass, also known as the "striper." These guys are like the cool kids of the fish world, with their sleek, silvery bodies and those bold black stripes running down their sides. They're like the aquatic version of a zebra—only way cooler.

Next, there's the rainbow trout. These guys are like nature's own little rainbow, with their vibrant hues of pink, green, and—you guessed it—rainbow. Plus, they've got those cute little speckles all over their bodies, like they've been splattered with paint by some artistic fish fairy.

And then there's the mighty muskellunge, or muskie for short. These are like the Arnold Schwarzeneggers of the fish world, with their massive size and fearsome reputation. They're like the action heroes of the underwater realm—you definitely don't want to mess with them.

Last but not least, let's not forget about the blue catfish. These guys have big, whiskered faces and a laid-back attitude. They're like the couch potatoes of the underwater world—content to just chill out and enjoy life.

Behavioral Signatures

Alright, let's take a peek at the world of fish behavior. Understanding how different species of fish behave is like having a secret decoder ring that unlocks the mysteries of the underwater world.

Understanding Species-Specific Behaviors

Each species of fish has its own unique set of behaviors, kind of like how each person has their own quirks and habits. Some fish like to hang out in schools, while others prefer to go solo. Some like to hide in rocky crevices, while others prefer to cruise along the sandy bottom. It's like they each have their own little personality—except instead of binge-watching Netflix, they're swimming around in the ocean.

So, how do you go about understanding these species-specific behaviors? Well, it's all about observation. Spend some time watching fish in their natural habitat, and you'll start to notice patterns. You'll see which fish like to hang out together, which ones are the bullies of the reef, and which ones are the shy introverts.

For example, take the clownfish. These guys are like the class clowns of the ocean—always goofing around and playing pranks on each other. They're known for their symbiotic relationship with sea anemones, which provide them with protection from predators. Watch a group of clownfish darting in and out of the tentacles of an anemone and you'll see just how playful and energetic they can be.

On the other hand, you've got the solitary hunters like the barracuda. These guys are like the lone wolves of the sea—sleek, stealthy, and always on the prowl. They'll lurk in the shadows, waiting for the perfect moment to strike, then dart out with lightning speed to nab their unsuspecting prey. It's like watching a scene straight out of a spy movie.

And let's not forget about the angelfish. These guys are like the social butterflies of the underwater world—always flitting about and mingling with the other fish. They'll form tight-knit schools and gracefully glide through the water in perfect synchrony. It's like watching a ballet performance, only with fins instead of tutus.

By observing these species-specific behaviors, you'll start to develop a deeper understanding of how fish interact with their environment and each other. You'll be able to anticipate their movements, predict their feeding habits, and even mimic their behavior to lure them into your fishing net. It's like becoming fluent in a whole new language—except instead of words, you're speaking fish.

Observing Schooling Patterns

I'm sure you have heard the term schooling before and have been intrigued by it especially since it's been used with respect to fishes and not kids. But what does it really mean? Schooling behavior is one of the most fascinating aspects of fish behavior and understanding it can be key to catching more fish on your next angling adventure.

Well, think of schooling like this: Fish are social creatures, just like humans. They like to hang out with their buddies, share gossip (okay, maybe not gossip), and watch each other's backs. By forming schools, fish can benefit from safety in numbers, making it harder for predators to single them out and snack on them for lunch.

But schooling isn't just about safety—it's also about efficiency. When fish swim together in a tight group, they create a hydrodynamic advantage that allows them to move through the water more efficiently, kind of like a NASCAR driver drafting behind another car. This allows them to conserve energy and cover more ground in search of food.

So, how can you observe schooling patterns in action? The first thing you'll notice is the sheer number of fish swimming together in a coordinated fashion. It's like watching a synchronized swimming routine, only with scales instead of swimsuits. They'll move in unison, darting and weaving through the water with impressive precision.

Next, pay attention to the shape and structure of the school. Some schools will form tight, compact balls, while others will spread out into long, sinuous lines. The shape of the school can give you clues about the species of fish you're dealing with and their behavior. For example, tightly packed schools are often composed of small, baitfish species like herring or sardines, while more loosely organized schools may indicate larger predatory fish like tuna or mackerel.

You'll also want to keep an eye out for any sudden changes in direction or speed. Fish schools are incredibly dynamic, with individuals constantly moving in and out of the group. These rapid changes in behavior can be triggered by a variety of factors, from the presence of predators to changes in water temperature or currents. By observing these changes, you can gain valuable insights into the behavior of the fish and adjust your fishing strategy accordingly.

You can use this knowledge to catch more fish. When you spot a school of fish, resist the urge to dive right in and start casting your line willy-nilly. Instead, take a moment to observe the behavior of the fish and assess the situation. Are they actively feeding, or are they just cruising along? Are they staying close to the surface, or are they holding deeper in the water column?

Once you've gathered this information, you can adjust your fishing tactics accordingly. If the fish are actively feeding near the surface, you might want to try casting topwater lures or surface flies to entice them into biting. If they're holding deeper in the water column, you might need to use sinking lures or weighted rigs to reach them.

Another thing to keep in mind is the size and type of baitfish that make up the school. Matching your bait to the size and color of the baitfish the fish are feeding on can dramatically increase your chances of success. After all, if you were a fish, wouldn't you be more likely to bite something that looks and smells like your favorite snack?

So, the next time you're out on the water and you spot a school of fish, take a moment to observe their behavior and adjust your fishing tactics accordingly.

Analyzing Feeding Behaviors

It's time to dive into the fascinating world of feeding behaviors—or, as I like to call it, "dinner time in the fish kingdom." Understanding how fish feed is crucial for any angler looking to reel in a big catch, so let's break it down.

First off, it's important to recognize that different species of fish have different feeding habits. Some are ambush predators, lurking in the shadows and pouncing on unsuspecting prey with lightning-fast reflexes. Others are more leisurely grazers, lazily munching on whatever tasty morsels happen to drift by. And then there are the scavengers, the bottom-dwellers who happily feast on whatever scraps they can scrounge up from the ocean floor.

So, how can you tell what kind of feeding behavior you're dealing with? Well, it all comes down to observation. Watch how the fish move and behave in their natural environment. Are they actively chasing down prey, or are they patiently waiting for something to come to them? Are they hunting alone, or are they working together in a coordinated effort?

Next, pay attention to the types of prey that the fish are targeting. Are they going after small baitfish, crustaceans, or insects? Are they feeding on the surface, in the middle of the water column, or down near the bottom? By understanding what the fish are eating and where they're feeding, you can better tailor your fishing tactics to match their preferences.

Now, let's talk about some common feeding behaviors that you might encounter out on the water. One of the most exciting feeding behaviors to witness is the "feeding frenzy," where fish go into a feeding frenzy and attack anything and everything in sight. This usually happens when there's an abundance of food in the water, like during a baitfish migration or a hatch of insects. When you see a feeding frenzy in action, it's like watching a piranha feeding frenzy—except hopefully without the sharp teeth and bloodshed.

Another common feeding behavior is "ambush predation," where fish lie in wait for their prey and then strike with lightning speed when it comes into range. This is a favorite tactic of predators like bass and pike, who use their stealth and agility to outsmart their prey. If you're targeting ambush predators, try using lures and baits that mimic injured or struggling prey to trigger a strike.

Then there's "bottom feeding," where fish scavenge for food on the ocean floor. This is a common feeding behavior among species like flounder, halibut, and catfish, who use their sensitive barbels to root around in the mud and sand in search of tasty treats. If you're targeting bottom feeders, try using bait rigs or bottom-bouncing lures to keep your bait close to the ocean floor where the fish are feeding.

Of course, these are just a few examples of the many feeding behaviors you might encounter while out on the water. The key is to observe the fish in their natural environment and adapt your fishing tactics accordingly.

Habitat Preferences

Understanding the importance of habitat in fish distribution is like knowing the best hangout spots in town—except instead of trendy cafes or cozy bars, we're talking about underwater real estate where fish like to chill.

Importance of Habitat in Fish Distribution

Think of habitat as a fish's home sweet home. Just like how you have your favorite spot on the couch or that perfect corner of your room where you feel most comfortable, fish have specific habitats where they thrive. These habitats provide everything fish need to survive and thrive, from food and shelter to the right temperature and oxygen levels.

Now, why does habitat matter so much when it comes to fish distribution? Well, it's simple—different species of fish have different preferences when it comes to where they live. Some fish like to hang out in shallow, weedy areas where they can hide from predators and ambush their prey. Others prefer deep, rocky habitats where they can find cooler temperatures and plenty of hiding spots.

But it's not just about what the habitat looks like—it's also about what's going on beneath the surface. Factors like water temperature, oxygen levels, and water clarity all play a role in determining which fish species will thrive in a particular habitat. For example, some fish species are more tolerant of low oxygen levels or high temperatures than others, so they'll be more likely to inhabit habitats where those conditions occur.

Another important factor to consider is the availability of food. Just like how you probably wouldn't want to live in a neighborhood with no grocery stores or restaurants, fish need access to plenty of food to survive. That's why you'll often find certain fish species congregating around areas with abundant food sources, like underwater vegetation or areas with strong currents that bring in lots of tasty treats.

Now, let's talk about the role that habitat plays in shaping fish communities. Different habitats support different communities of fish, each adapted to thrive in its specific environment. For example, a river with fast-moving currents and rocky bottoms might be home to species like trout and smallmouth bass, while a shallow, weedy lake might be teeming with panfish like bluegill and crappie.

Understanding habitat preferences is also crucial for conservation efforts. By identifying and protecting important fish habitats, we can help ensure the long-term health and sustainability of fish populations. This might involve restoring degraded habitats, creating artificial habitats like underwater reefs or fish attractors, or implementing regulations to protect critical habitat areas from development or pollution.

In conclusion, habitat preferences play a vital role in determining the distribution of fish species. By understanding the importance of habitat in fish distribution, anglers can increase their chances of success by targeting areas where their preferred species are likely to be found.

Identifying Prime Locations

Picture this: You're on a fishing adventure, armed with your favorite rod and reel, ready to reel in the big one. But wait—where should you cast your line? Identifying prime fishing locations is like solving a mystery, and the clues lie beneath the surface of the water.

One key to unlocking the mystery of fish location is identifying prime fishing locations—those hidden hotspots where fish are likely to congregate. These locations act as fish magnets, drawing in all kinds of species with their irresistible charm.

Let's start with submerged structures. These underwater hideaways are like luxury condos for fish, providing shelter, shade, and a place to hang out with friends. Submerged structures can include fallen trees, submerged rocks, or even artificial reefs. These structures create a complex underwater habitat where fish can hide from predators, ambush prey, and take refuge from strong currents.

Drop-offs are another prime location for fish, offering a change in depth that attracts a variety of species. Picture a fish highway—drop-offs are like on-ramps and off-ramps, providing easy access to deeper water where fish can find cooler temperatures and abundant food. Drop-offs can occur along the shoreline, where shallow water suddenly plunges into deeper depths, or in the middle of a lake or river, where underwater contours create depth changes.

But what about weed beds? These underwater gardens are a favorite hangout spot for many fish species, offering shelter, food, and a place to spawn. Weed beds provide cover from predators and serve as a buffet for hungry fish, attracting everything from bass and pike to panfish like bluegill and crappie. Fishing around weed beds can be tricky—you'll need to navigate through the vegetation without getting tangled up, but the payoff can be well worth it when you hook into a big one.

Now, let's talk tactics.

- When fishing around submerged structures, try casting your bait or lure near the edges of the structure, where fish are likely to be lurking. Pay attention to any changes in the underwater terrain—fish often congregate near points, bends, or other features that create current breaks or ambush points.

- When fishing drop-offs, target the transition zone between shallow and deep water, where fish are most likely to be feeding. This might involve casting your line parallel to the drop-off or jigging your bait or lure along the edge of the depth change.

- And when fishing weed beds, focus on the edges or openings in the vegetation, where fish are most likely to be feeding. Weedless lures or rigs can help prevent snagging on the thick vegetation, allowing you to fish with confidence in even the weediest of waters.

In conclusion, identifying prime fishing locations like submerged structures, drop-offs, and weed beds is essential for anglers looking to maximize their success on the water. By understanding the characteristics of these habitats and employing the right tactics, anglers can increase their chances of hooking into a trophy fish.

Examples of Ideal Habitats for Different Species

- First up, let's talk about bass. These feisty fish are notorious for lurking around submerged structures like fallen trees, brush piles, and rocky outcrops. Bass love to ambush their prey from the shadows, using these structures as cover to sneak up on unsuspecting baitfish. If you're targeting bass, focus your efforts around these underwater hideouts, casting your bait or lure near the edges where bass are likely to be waiting in ambush.

- Next on the list, we have trout. These sleek swimmers are often found in cool, clear streams and rivers, where they prefer fast-flowing water with plenty of oxygen and cover. Look for trout in riffles, runs, and pools, where they can find refuge from the current and easy access to food. Trout are also fond of structure, so keep an eye out for submerged rocks, fallen logs, and undercut banks—these are prime spots to hook into a trophy trout.

- Moving on to panfish like bluegill and crappie, these freshwater favorites are often found around weed beds, submerged vegetation, and other underwater structures. Bluegill, in particular, love to hang out near the edges of weed beds, where they can find shelter and abundant food. Crappie, on the other hand, are more likely to be found around submerged timber, brush piles, or boat docks, where they can find cover and ambush passing prey.

- Now, let's shift our focus to saltwater species like redfish and snook. These hard-fighting fish are often found in coastal waters, where they patrol the shorelines, flats, and mangrove-lined creeks in search of food. Redfish are especially fond of shallow flats and oyster beds, where they can root around for crabs, shrimp, and other tasty treats. Snooks, on the other hand, prefer deeper channels and tidal creeks, where they can find refuge from predators and ambush passing baitfish.

- Last but not least, let's talk about offshore species like tuna, mahi-mahi, and billfish. These oceanic giants are often found around underwater structures like reefs, wrecks, and seamounts, where they can find food and shelter. Tuna, in particular, are known for congregating around temperature breaks and current edges, where they can find an abundance of baitfish. Mahi-mahi, on the other hand, are often found around floating debris, weed lines, and offshore buoys, where they can find shelter and food.

By targeting these prime spots and using the right tactics, anglers can increase their chances of hooking into their target species and enjoying a memorable day on the water. So, the next time you're planning a fishing trip, take some time to research the habitats of your target species—it could make all the difference between a successful outing and a day of frustration.

Seasonal Migrations

Alright, folks, let's talk about one of the most fascinating aspects of fish behavior: seasonal migrations. Just like snowbirds fleeing the cold for warmer climates, many fish species have their own seasonal patterns of movement that are driven by changes in temperature, water levels, and food availability. Understanding these migrations is like having a treasure map of the underwater world—it can lead you straight to the motherlode of fish.

Following Seasonal Patterns

First off, let's discuss the spring migration. As temperatures start to warm up and daylight hours lengthen, many fish species begin their journey from deep wintering grounds to shallow spawning areas. This is prime time for anglers to target spawning fish like bass, crappie, and walleye, as they move into shallow bays, tributaries, and flats to reproduce. By targeting these spawning areas during the spring migration, anglers can capitalize on the abundance of hungry fish and enjoy some epic fishing action.

As we move into the summer months, fish migrations continue, albeit in a different direction. With water temperatures on the rise, many fish species seek out cooler, deeper waters to escape the heat. This often means heading toward deeper channels, offshore reefs, and underwater structures where they can find relief from the summer sun. Anglers targeting species like trout, salmon, and striped bass may need to adjust their tactics accordingly, focusing their efforts on deeper water and using techniques like trolling or jigging to entice bites.

Come fall, it's time for the annual migration of baitfish and their predators. As water temperatures start to cool down and daylight hours shorten, baitfish begin their journey from shallow feeding grounds to deeper wintering areas. This mass exodus of baitfish triggers a feeding frenzy among predatory species like bass, pike, and muskie, as they follow the baitfish in search of an easy meal. For anglers, this means targeting areas where baitfish are concentrated, such as points, shoals, and drop-offs, and using techniques like casting crankbaits or jigging spoons to mimic the movements of fleeing baitfish.

Last but not least, we have the winter migration. As temperatures plummet and ice begins to form on the surface of lakes and rivers, many fish species head for deeper waters in search of warmer temperatures and more stable conditions. This often means hunkering down near underwater structures like submerged timber, rock piles, and deep holes, where they can find refuge from the cold and access to food. For ice anglers, this presents a unique opportunity to target fish in their wintering grounds, using techniques like jigging or tip-ups to entice strikes from lethargic fish.

In conclusion, understanding the seasonal migrations of fish is essential for anglers looking to stay one step ahead of their quarry. By following these seasonal patterns and adjusting their tactics accordingly, anglers can increase their chances of success and enjoy a rewarding day on the water, no matter what time of year it is. So, the next time you're planning a fishing trip, take some time to research the seasonal migrations of your target species—it could be the key to unlocking some epic fishing action.

Spawning Seasons and Migration Routes

When it comes to fish, reproduction is a crucial part of their life cycle, and understanding spawning seasons and migration routes is key to unlocking their behavior.

First things first, let's talk about spawning seasons. For many fish species, spawning is a once-a-year event that occurs during specific times and under specific conditions. These conditions often include water temperature, daylight hours, and lunar cycles. In freshwater, spawning typically occurs in the spring when water temperatures start to rise, triggering the instinct for fish to reproduce. During this time, fish like bass, crappie, and walleye migrate from deeper wintering areas to shallow, protected spawning grounds like tributaries, flats, and gravel beds. Once they've found a suitable spawning location, males and females engage in courtship rituals before releasing their eggs and sperm into the water, where fertilization takes place. This is an incredibly vulnerable time for fish, as they are focused on reproduction and may be less wary of predators, making them easier targets for anglers.

Now, let's talk about migration routes. Just like any journey, fish migrations require careful planning and navigation. Migration routes are often influenced by a variety of factors, including food availability, water temperature, and habitat structure. In freshwater, migration routes can vary depending on the species and the time of year. For example, during the spring migration, fish may follow tributaries and river systems upstream to reach spawning grounds, while during the fall migration, they may move downstream in search of deeper, warmer water. In saltwater, migration routes can be even more complex, with fish traveling long distances along coastlines, across the open ocean, and even between different ocean basins. Species like salmon, tuna, and billfish are known for their epic migrations, covering thousands of miles in search of food, spawning grounds, or more favorable environmental conditions.

Understanding spawning seasons and migration routes is essential for anglers looking to target specific species at the right time and place. By knowing when and where fish are likely to spawn or migrate, anglers can plan their fishing trips accordingly, increasing their chances of success and ensuring a memorable day on the water.

Impact on Fishing Strategies

Now that we've covered spawning seasons and migration routes, let's explore how these phenomena impact fishing strategies. Understanding the seasonal movements of fish is crucial for anglers looking to maximize their success on the water.

During spawning seasons, fish become more predictable in their behavior, as their primary focus shifts to reproduction. This can present both opportunities and challenges for anglers. On one hand, spawning fish tend to congregate in specific areas, making them easier to locate. For example, bass may gather around shallow beds or brush piles, while salmon and steelhead might congregate in river riffles or gravel bars. By targeting these spawning grounds, anglers can increase their chances of encountering fish.

On the other hand, spawning fish can also be more selective in their feeding habits and less aggressive in their strikes. This means that anglers may need to adjust their tactics accordingly. For example, finesse techniques like drop-shotting or jigging may be more effective than aggressive techniques like topwater lures or crankbaits. Additionally, anglers may need to use lighter line and smaller hooks to avoid spooking wary fish.

In addition to spawning seasons, migration routes also play a significant role in determining fishing strategies. When fish are on the move, anglers must adapt their tactics to intercept them along their migration routes. This requires careful planning and a good understanding of the local geography and habitat.

For example, during the spring migration, many fish species move from deeper wintering areas to shallow spawning grounds. Anglers can take advantage of this movement by targeting key migration routes such as tributaries, river channels, and shoreline transitions. By positioning themselves along these routes, anglers can intercept migrating fish as they move upstream.

Similarly, during the fall migration, fish may move from shallow spawning grounds to deeper wintering areas. Anglers can target these migration routes by focusing on deeper holes, channels, and underwater structures where fish are likely to congregate. Trolling or drifting along these routes with live bait or artificial lures can be highly effective for catching migrating fish.

In addition to spawning seasons and migration routes, anglers must also consider other factors that can impact fishing strategies, such as weather conditions, water temperature, and time of day. For example, fish may be more active during low-light conditions like dawn and dusk, or during periods of stable weather. By timing their fishing trips to coincide with these optimal conditions, anglers can increase their chances of success.

Furthermore, anglers must be prepared to adapt their tactics on the fly based on changing conditions. This may involve switching baits, adjusting presentation techniques, or moving to different locations to find active fish. Flexibility is key when it comes to fishing, and the ability to read the water and make informed decisions in real time can make all the difference between a successful day on the water and a frustrating one.

Water Temperature and Conditions

Let's talk about water temperature and how it influences the behavior of our aquatic friends. Fish may not have weather apps on their phones, but they're incredibly tuned in to changes in water temperature. Just like us reaching for a jacket when it gets chilly, fish react to shifts in water temperature by adjusting their behavior.

Influence of Water Temperature on Fish Behavior

First off, let's tackle the basics. Warmer water typically means more active fish. In warmer temperatures, fish metabolism speeds up, and they become more energetic and hungrier. This means they'll be more willing to chase down a tasty lure or bait. On the flip side, when the water gets chilly, fish tend to slow down. Their metabolism decreases, and they become less active and more lethargic. So, if you're fishing in colder conditions, you might need to slow down your presentation to entice those sluggish fish.

But it's not just about the overall temperature—fish are also sensitive to changes in water temperature. A sudden drop or rise in temperature can send fish scattering or trigger feeding frenzies, depending on the circumstances. For example, a sudden cold front might send fish seeking refuge in deeper, warmer waters, while a warm spell in the winter could trigger a burst of activity as fish take advantage of the temporary warmth.

Water temperature also plays a role in determining where fish hang out. Different species have different temperature preferences, so knowing the temperature ranges preferred by your target species can help you narrow down your search. For example, trout prefer cooler waters, so they'll often be found in streams or lakes with colder temperatures, while bass are more tolerant of warmer waters.

Another factor to consider is how water temperature affects the availability of oxygen. Warmer water holds less oxygen than cooler water, so as temperatures rise, fish may seek out areas with higher oxygen levels, such as near the surface or in areas with flowing water. This can impact where you'll find fish in a body of water—for example, during hot summer days, you might have more luck fishing in shaded areas or near inflowing streams where oxygen levels are higher.

In addition to temperature, water clarity can also influence fish behavior. Clear water allows fish to see more clearly and may make them more wary of approaching lures or baits. On the other hand, murky water can provide cover for ambush predators like bass and pike, who rely on stealth to catch their prey.

So, what's an angler to do with all this information? Paying attention to water temperature and conditions is not just about being aware—it's about using that knowledge to your advantage on the water. When you're faced with warmer temperatures, it's time to dial up the action. Try using faster-moving lures or baits that mimic the frantic activity of baitfish, enticing those energized fish to strike. Think about it—if you were a fish feeling the warmth of the sun on your scales, wouldn't you be more inclined to chase down a meal in the warmer water?

On the flip side, when the mercury drops and the water temperature takes a plunge, it's time to slow things down. Cold-blooded creatures like fish are highly attuned to changes in temperature, and when the water gets chilly, they're not exactly in a hurry to burn calories. Instead, they'll be seeking out areas where they can conserve energy and stay warm. This means you'll want to present your lures or baits in a more subtle and enticing manner, giving those lethargic fish a chance to strike without expending too much energy.

But adjusting your tactics doesn't stop there. In colder temperatures, fish are also more likely to seek out areas where they can find warmth and shelter. This might mean targeting shallow bays or areas with submerged structures where the water temperature is slightly higher or focusing on areas with vegetation or rocky cover where fish can hide from predators and conserve heat. By thinking like a fish and targeting these key areas, you'll increase your chances of hooking into a trophy catch even when the temperature drops.

Understanding Water Clarity and Oxygen Levels

Water clarity and oxygen levels—two crucial factors that can make or break your day on the water. So, let's take a closer look.

First up, water clarity. Picture this: you're peering into the depths, trying to spot that telltale flash of a fish below. But if the water is murky or stained, your chances of spotting your target are significantly reduced. That's because visibility is key when it comes to fishing success. In clear water, fish rely on their keen eyesight to spot prey and avoid predators, so they may be more cautious and selective about what they eat. On the other hand, in murky or stained water, fish may rely more on their other senses, like smell and vibration, to detect food. This means you'll need to adjust your presentation accordingly—think about using baits or lures that produce strong vibrations or emit scent to attract fish in these conditions.

But water clarity isn't just about visibility—it also plays a role in how light penetrates the water column. In clear water, sunlight can penetrate deeper, warming the water and providing energy for aquatic plants to grow. This can create a prime habitat for fish, as they'll be drawn to areas with abundant food sources like algae and aquatic insects. On the flip side, in murky water, light penetration is limited, which can lead to cooler temperatures and reduced plant growth. In these conditions, fish may seek out areas with structure or cover, like fallen trees or submerged brush piles, where they can ambush prey and avoid predators.

Now, let's talk about oxygen levels. Just like you and me, fish need oxygen to survive. And while they may have gills to extract oxygen from the water, they still rely on adequate oxygen levels to thrive. So, what happens when oxygen levels drop? Well, let's just say it's not good news for our aquatic friends. Low oxygen levels can stress fish out, making them more susceptible to disease and less likely to feed. In extreme cases, it can even lead to fish kills, where large numbers of fish die off due to lack of oxygen.

But here's where it gets interesting—oxygen levels aren't always uniform throughout the water column. In fact, they can vary significantly depending on a variety of factors, including temperature, wind, and the presence of aquatic plants. For example, warm water holds less oxygen than cold water, so during the summer months, fish may seek out cooler, oxygen-rich areas like deep holes or shaded areas. Similarly, wind can create surface turbulence, which can help oxygenate the water and create feeding opportunities for fish.

Identifying Productive Fishing Spots Based on Conditions

Alright, let's get down to the nitty-gritty of finding those prime fishing spots based on water conditions. You've got your gear all set up, you're armed with knowledge about water clarity and oxygen levels—now it's time to pinpoint those areas where the fish are just waiting to bite.

Fish love structure—it provides shelter, ambush points, and a buffet of food sources. So, when you're scouting for productive fishing spots, keep an eye out for anything that breaks up the monotony of the underwater landscape. Fallen trees, submerged rocks, weed beds, and underwater ledges are all prime examples of structures that can hold fish. These areas provide cover for fish to hide from predators and wait for unsuspecting prey to swim by.

Next up, let's talk about current. Rivers and streams are like aquatic highways for fish, and they'll often congregate in areas where the current is just right. Look for places where the current slows down, like eddies, bends in the river, or behind large rocks. These areas provide a break from the relentless flow of the water, allowing fish to conserve energy while still having access to food. Plus, the slower current makes it easier for fish to ambush passing prey, making these spots a hotspot for hungry predators.

Now, let's talk about transitions. Fish are creatures of habit, and they'll often hang out where one type of habitat transitions into another. This could be where a rocky shoreline meets a sandy bottom, where a shallow flat drops off into deeper water, or where a weed bed meets open water. These transition zones act like natural feeding lanes, funneling prey into areas where fish are waiting to strike. So, keep an eye out for these subtle changes in the underwater landscape—they could be the key to unlocking some seriously productive fishing spots.

And let's not forget about depth. Fish, like humans, have their preferred comfort zones when it comes to water depth. Some species prefer shallow water where they can bask in the warmth of the sun and hunt for food near the surface. Others prefer deeper water where they can escape the heat of the day and ambush passing prey in the cool depths.

Lastly, let's talk about cover. Fish love cover—it gives them a sense of security and helps them avoid predators. Look for areas with overhanging trees, submerged brush piles, or floating vegetation. These areas provide shade, shelter, and a smorgasbord of food sources for hungry fish. Plus, they can be less heavily fished than more obvious spots, giving you a better chance of hooking into some quality fish.

River Fishing Strategies

Alright, fellow angler, let's talk rivers! Rivers are like the highways of the aquatic world—bustling with life and full of surprises around every bend. But navigating these watery thoroughfares requires a bit of finesse and an understanding of their unique dynamics. So, grab your fishing rod and let's embark on a journey down the river of knowledge.

Dynamics of River Environments

First off, there's the current. Current is the lifeblood of rivers, shaping the landscape and dictating the movement of fish. Fast-moving currents create oxygen-rich environments that fish love, while slower currents provide shelter and hiding spots. So, when you're fishing in rivers, pay close attention to the speed and direction of the current. Look for areas where the current slows down, like eddies, bends in the river, or behind large rocks. These are prime spots for fish to hang out and wait for passing prey.

Then there's structure. Rivers are chock-full of structures, from fallen trees and submerged logs to rocky outcrops and undercut banks. These features provide shelter, ambush points, and a buffet of food sources for hungry fish. So, when you're fishing in rivers, keep an eye out for anything that breaks up the monotony of the underwater landscape. Cast your line near submerged logs or under overhanging branches, and you might just hook into a monster fish hiding in the shadows.

Now, let's talk about depth. Rivers come in all shapes and sizes, from shallow, meandering streams to deep, powerful rapids. Different species of fish prefer different depths, so it's important to target areas that match the preferences of your target species. In general, deeper pools and runs tend to hold larger fish, while shallow riffles and runs are home to smaller, more agile species. When you're fishing in rivers, pay attention to the depth of the water and adjust your tactics accordingly.

And let's not forget about cover. You already know that fish love cover. Look for areas with submerged vegetation, fallen trees, or rocky outcrops. These areas provide shelter, shade, and a smorgasbord of food sources for hungry fish. Plus, they can be less heavily fished than more obvious spots, giving you a better chance of hooking into some quality fish.

Now, let's talk about the ever-changing nature of rivers. Rivers are dynamic and constantly evolving, with water levels and currents fluctuating with the seasons. This means that what worked yesterday might not work today, so it's important to stay adaptable and be willing to change up your tactics on the fly. Keep an eye on water levels, weather forecasts, and local fishing reports to stay one step ahead of the game.

And last but not least, let's talk about safety. Rivers can be unpredictable and unforgiving, with fast-moving currents and hidden hazards lurking beneath the surface. Always wear a life jacket, watch your footing, and never wade into unfamiliar waters without proper equipment and knowledge. And remember, it's always better to be safe than sorry—no fish is worth risking your life for.

Locating Fish in Varying Currents

Let's delve deeper into the world of river fishing and tackle the challenge of locating fish in varying currents. Rivers are dynamic environments, with currents ranging from gentle ripples to powerful rapids, and each presents its own set of opportunities and obstacles for anglers.

We should start the conversation with eddies. Eddies are areas of water that flow in the opposite direction of the main current, often forming behind obstructions like rocks or fallen trees. These swirling pockets of water create a calm refuge for fish, offering a respite from the relentless pull of the current. When fishing in eddies, target the seam where the fast-moving current meets the slower-moving water, as this is where fish are most likely to be feeding. Cast your line upstream and let it drift naturally into the eddy, keeping an eye out for any subtle strikes or tugs on your line.

Next up, let's talk about riffles. Riffles are shallow, rocky stretches of water where the current flows over a series of small obstacles, creating a turbulent surface. While riffles may not seem like prime fishing spots at first glance, they can actually be incredibly productive, especially for species like trout and smallmouth bass. Fish love to hang out in the seams and pockets between rocks, where they can ambush passing prey and take advantage of the abundant insect life that thrives in riffle habitats. When fishing in riffles, focus your efforts on these areas of calm water, and don't be afraid to experiment with different presentations and techniques to entice the fish into biting.

Moving on, let's talk about runs. Runs are deeper, faster-moving stretches of water that connect pools and riffles, and they're often overlooked by anglers in favor of more obvious fishing spots. However, runs can be incredibly productive, especially during periods of heightened activity like feeding or spawning. Look for areas of the run where the current slows down, such as the inside bend of a meander or the tailout of a pool, as these are natural gathering spots for fish. Cast your line upstream and let it drift naturally through the run, keeping an eye out for any subtle strikes or movements in the water.

And let's not forget about pools. Pools are deep, slow-moving stretches of water that provide fish with a refuge from the fast-flowing currents of the river. They're often found below riffles or runs, where the water deepens and slows down, creating a calm, serene environment that fish love. Pools are prime feeding and resting spots for fish, especially during the heat of the day when the sun is high and the water is warm. Look for areas of the pool where the current is minimal, such as the head and tail of the pool, as these are natural gathering spots for fish. Cast your line into these areas and let it sink naturally to the bottom, where the fish are likely to be lurking.

In conclusion, locating fish in varying currents requires a combination of patience, observation, and a keen understanding of river dynamics.

Strategies for Changing Conditions

So, you've got your waders on, your rod in hand, and you're ready to conquer the ever-changing currents of the river. But what happens when Mother Nature throws you a curveball and the conditions suddenly shift? Don't worry because I've got some strategies up my sleeve to help you navigate any changes the river may throw your way.

Let's start with a classic scenario: a sudden rise or drop in water levels. This can happen for a variety of reasons, from heavy rain upstream to dam releases or snowmelt. When faced with fluctuating water levels, the key is to adapt quickly and adjust your fishing tactics accordingly. In high water conditions, fish tend to seek out areas of refuge where the current is slower and the water is calmer, such as eddies, backwaters, or the inside bends of the river. Target these areas with larger, more visible lures or baits that can grab the attention of fish despite the murky conditions.

Conversely, in low water conditions, fish may become more concentrated in deeper pools and runs, where the water is cooler and oxygen levels are higher. Look for areas of the river where the current is still strong, such as the tailouts of pools or the heads of riffles, as these spots can act as natural funnels for fish moving upstream. Switch to smaller, more finesse presentations like nymphs or small streamers, and focus your efforts on making precise casts to likely holding spots.

Next up, let's talk about changes in water clarity. Whether it's due to a sudden influx of sediment from upstream runoff or a bout of windy weather stirring up the bottom, murky water can pose a challenge for anglers. In these conditions, it's important to rely on your other senses, such as sound and feel, to detect strikes and bites. Opt for lures or baits with bright colors or exaggerated movements that can attract fish despite the reduced visibility, and consider using scent or noise-producing attractants to help fish locate your offering.

On the flip side, clear water conditions can be equally challenging, as fish become more wary and easily spooked by any unnatural movements or disturbances. In these situations, it's essential to downsize your tackle and use stealthy, finesse presentations to avoid detection. Lighter line, smaller hooks, and natural-looking baits or flies are all key components of a successful approach in clear water, along with making long, accurate casts to avoid spooking wary fish.

And let's not forget about changes in weather patterns. Whether it's a sudden cold front moving in, a shift in wind direction, or a change in barometric pressure, weather can have a significant impact on fish behavior. In general, fish tend to become more active and feed more aggressively ahead of a storm front or other weather system, so it's often worth braving the elements to capitalize on these feeding frenzies. Look for areas of the river where the current is strongest, such as riffles, runs, or the heads of pools, and target these spots with fast-moving lures or baits that can trigger a reaction strike from hungry fish.

In conclusion, the key to success in river fishing is flexibility and adaptability. By staying attuned to changes in water levels, clarity, and weather patterns, and adjusting your tactics accordingly, you can increase your chances of hooking into some trophy-worthy fish, no matter what the river throws your way.

Lake and Pond Tactics

Lakes and ponds—perfect for a leisurely day of fishing and maybe a picnic or two. But before you cast your line, let's take a closer look at the diverse habitats you'll encounter beneath the surface.

Diverse Habitats in Lakes and Ponds

Lakes and ponds may seem uniform from above, but beneath the water lies a world of varied habitats, each with its own unique characteristics and fish species.

First up, we've got the shoreline structures. Think fallen trees, submerged brush piles, and overhanging vegetation—basically, all the places where fish like to hang out and ambush their prey. These areas provide ample cover and shade for fish to hide and wait for unsuspecting prey. Plus, they're a haven for aquatic insects and small baitfish, making them prime feeding grounds for larger predators. So, next time you're fishing a lake or pond, be sure to target these shoreline structures with your lures or baits and get ready for some explosive strikes.

Moving out from the shoreline, we've got the shallow flats and weed beds. These areas are like underwater jungles, teeming with life and activity. The shallow water and abundant sunlight promote the growth of aquatic plants, which in turn provide food and shelter for a wide variety of fish species. Look for pockets and openings within the weed beds, as these are often ambush points for predatory fish waiting to pounce on passing prey. And don't be afraid to get your lure or bait right in the thick of it—sometimes, that's where the biggest fish are hiding.

Now, let's talk about the deep basins and drop-offs. These are the underwater highways that fish use to move between feeding and resting areas, and they're like the express lanes of the lake or pond. Drop-offs can vary in depth and steepness, from gradual slopes to sheer cliffs, but they all serve the same purpose: to provide fish with access to deeper water and cooler temperatures. Target these areas with your lures or baits, especially during the warmer months when fish may seek refuge from the heat in the depths below.

And let's not forget about the open water areas. Sure, they may seem barren at first glance, but don't be fooled—these areas can hold some surprising secrets. Look for submerged humps, points, and submerged islands, as these features can attract and concentrate fish in otherwise featureless expanses of water. Don't be afraid to cover some ground in search of active fish—trolling or drifting with your lures or baits can be an effective way to locate fish in open water areas.

Last but not least, we have the aquatic vegetation. Whether it's lily pads, hydrillas, or milfoils, aquatic plants provide vital habitat for fish and other aquatic organisms. Fish use these areas for spawning, feeding, and seeking shelter from predators, so they're definitely worth targeting during your fishing adventures. Just be prepared to navigate through the thick vegetation, and don't be surprised if you come face-to-face with a few frogs or turtles along the way!

Targeting Fish in Shoreline Structures and Deep Basins

Now that we've covered the diverse habitats of lakes and ponds, let's delve deeper into how to target fish in shoreline structures and deep basins, and how to adapt your strategies to seasonal changes.

When it comes to shoreline structures, such as fallen trees, submerged brush piles, and overhanging vegetation, timing is key. During the warmer months, fish tend to move into shallower water to feed and spawn, making these areas prime targets for anglers. Topwater lures and shallow-running crankbaits are excellent choices for targeting fish in shoreline structures during this time, as they mimic the movements of baitfish and insects on the water's surface.

As the seasons change and water temperatures begin to drop, fish will start to move into deeper water in search of warmer temperatures and food sources. This is where deep basins and drop-offs come into play. Jigging spoons, blade baits, and soft plastics are effective lures for targeting fish in deeper water, as they can be worked vertically to imitate dying baitfish or bottom-dwelling prey. Additionally, trolling deep-diving crankbaits along the edges of drop-offs can be a productive strategy for enticing fish in these areas.

Now, let's talk about adapting your strategies to seasonal changes. During the spring months, fish are typically more active and aggressive as they prepare for spawning. Targeting shallow shoreline structures and casting shallow-running crankbaits or spinnerbaits can yield excellent results during this time. As summer approaches and water temperatures rise, fish may become more lethargic and seek refuge in deeper, cooler water. Transitioning to deeper water tactics, such as jigging or trolling, can help you continue to catch fish as the seasons change.

As fall sets in and water temperatures begin to cool, fish will start to feed heavily in preparation for the winter months. Shallow shoreline structures become prime feeding grounds once again, as fish move back into shallower water to fatten up before the cold sets in. Crankbaits, spinnerbaits, and jerkbaits can be effective lures for targeting fish in these areas during the fall months. Finally, as winter arrives and water temperatures drop, fish will become more sluggish and less active. Targeting deeper water near drop-offs and channel edges with slow-moving lures or live bait can be your best bet for enticing bites during the colder months.

Saltwater Hotspots

Buckle up your life jackets because we're about to set sail into the vast and mysterious world of saltwater fishing! The ocean, my friends, is like a giant playground for anglers, with endless opportunities to reel in some trophy-worthy catches. But before we cast our lines, let's take a closer look at what makes saltwater fishing so exciting and challenging.

Exploring the Vastness of the Ocean

Let's start with the sheer size of the ocean. I mean, we're talking about covering more ground than a marathon runner on steroids! With its vast expanse of open water, navigating the ocean can be like trying to find a needle in a haystack. But don't worry—where there's water, there are fish, and where there are fish, there are hotspots waiting to be discovered.

Now, when it comes to exploring the ocean, there are a few key factors to keep in mind. Tidal movements, coastal structures, and offshore adventures all play a role in determining where the fish are hiding. Tides, for example, can cause currents that concentrate baitfish and other prey, attracting larger predatory fish to the area. So, pay attention to the tides, folks, because they can make or break your fishing trip! We will talk more about them in the next section.

Coastal structures, such as jetties, reefs, and rock formations, provide valuable habitat for a variety of saltwater species. These structures create shelter and feeding opportunities for fish, making them prime targets for anglers.

And that is not all because there's more! Offshore adventures offer a whole new world of fishing opportunities for those brave enough to venture beyond the safety of the shoreline. From chasing big game fish like marlin and tuna to bottom fishing for snapper and grouper, the open ocean is a treasure trove of angling excitement. Just be sure to pack some extra sunscreen and seasickness medication, because things can get a little rough out there!

Now, let's talk tactics. When exploring saltwater hotspots, it's important to keep an open mind and be willing to adapt your fishing strategies to the conditions at hand. If you're targeting pelagic species like mahi-mahi or wahoo, trolling with artificial lures or rigged baits can be highly effective. On the other hand, if you're bottom fishing for reef dwellers like snapper or grouper, dropping down a live bait or jigging with a weighted lure can entice even the most stubborn fish to bite.

And let's not forget about the importance of gear. When fishing in the open ocean, you'll need to outfit yourself with sturdy rods, heavy-duty reels, and strong line to handle the powerful fish you're likely to encounter. And don't skimp on the terminal tackle either—quality hooks, swivels, and leaders can mean the difference between landing a trophy fish and watching it swim away.

Understanding Tidal Movements and Coastal Structures

Now, when we talk about tidal movements, we're referring to the ebb and flow of the ocean's tides, which are caused by the gravitational pull of the moon and the sun. These tidal movements create currents that can have a significant impact on fish behavior and feeding patterns. For example, during incoming tides, nutrient-rich water is pushed into coastal areas, attracting baitfish and other prey species. This, in turn, draws in larger predatory fish looking for an easy meal. So, if you're looking to reel in some big catches, it's important to pay attention to the tides and fish accordingly.

But tidal movements aren't the only thing you need to consider when fishing in saltwater—coastal structures also play a crucial role in determining where the fish are hiding. Coastal structures, such as jetties, reefs, and rock formations, provide valuable habitat for a wide variety of saltwater species. These structures create shelter from strong currents and waves, as well as provide feeding opportunities for fish. So, if you're looking to target specific species, it's important to familiarize yourself with the coastal structures in your area and understand how they influence fish behavior.

For example, rocky shorelines and jetties are prime spots for targeting species like snook and redfish, which often use these structures as ambush points to prey on passing baitfish. Similarly, coral reefs and underwater rock formations are hotspots for a variety of reef-dwelling species, including snapper, grouper, and triggerfish. By understanding the relationship between tidal movements and coastal structures, you can pinpoint the most productive fishing spots and increase your chances of success on the water.

Now, let's talk tactics. When fishing around tidal movements and coastal structures, it's important to adapt your fishing strategies to the conditions at hand. For example, during incoming tides, predatory fish are often more active and aggressive, making it an ideal time to target them with fast-moving lures or live baits. On the other hand, during outgoing tides, fish may seek shelter in calmer waters near coastal structures, making it a prime opportunity for bottom fishing or casting around structures.

When it comes to fishing around coastal structures, presentation is key. Fish are often found hiding in the shadows of rocks and reefs, waiting to ambush passing prey. So, be sure to cast your bait or lure close to the structure and work it slowly and methodically through the strike zone. Pay attention to any changes in water depth or current flow, as these can indicate potential feeding areas or ambush points.

And let's not forget about safety. When fishing around coastal structures, it's important to exercise caution and be aware of your surroundings. Rocks and reefs can be slippery and sharp, so watch your step and wear appropriate footwear. Additionally, be mindful of changing tides and currents, which can quickly sweep you away from shore if you're not careful.

Offshore Adventures for Saltwater Angling

Now, offshore fishing is a whole different ball game compared to fishing inshore or near coastal structures. When you venture into offshore waters, you're entering the domain of some of the ocean's most prized game fish, including marlin, tuna, mahi-mahi, and more. But before you set sail, it's essential to be prepared and equipped for the challenges that await you on the open sea.

Offshore fishing can be unpredictable and potentially hazardous, so it's crucial to prioritize safety above all else. Make sure your boat is in top-notch condition and equipped with all the necessary safety gear, including life jackets, flares, a VHF radio, and an emergency locator beacon. Additionally, familiarize yourself with local regulations and weather conditions before heading offshore, and always keep a close eye on the forecast to avoid getting caught in rough seas or inclement weather.

When it comes to offshore angling, one of the keys to success is covering as much water as possible to locate the fish. Unlike inshore or coastal fishing, where you may be targeting specific structures or feeding areas, offshore fish can be found roaming vast expanses of open water. So, it's essential to have a game plan and be prepared to adapt your tactics based on the conditions you encounter.

One popular offshore fishing technique is trolling, where you tow baits or lures behind your boat at varying depths and speeds to entice hungry predators. Trolling allows you to cover a lot of ground and search for actively feeding fish, making it an effective strategy for targeting species like marlin, tuna, and wahoo. Just be sure to vary your trolling speed and patterns to mimic the movement of natural prey and increase your chances of hooking into a trophy fish.

Another offshore angling tactic is bottom fishing, where you drop baited rigs or lures to the ocean floor in search of reef-dwelling species like grouper, snapper, and amberjack. Bottom fishing can be highly productive, especially around underwater structures like reefs, wrecks, and oil rigs, which attract a variety of bottom-dwelling species. Just be prepared to wrestle with some hefty fish and have your drag set accordingly!

And let's not forget about live baiting, which involves using live baitfish or squid to entice hungry predators into striking. Live baiting can be particularly effective for species like kingfish, mahi-mahi, and sailfish, which are known for their aggressive feeding habits. Keep your live baits lively and swimming naturally to maximize their appeal to passing predators, and be ready for some heart-pounding strikes when the action heats up!

Of course, no offshore fishing adventure would be complete without some epic battles with trophy-worthy fish. Whether you're tangling with a massive marlin on the end of your line or battling a feisty tuna as it runs circles around your boat, there's nothing quite like the thrill of offshore angling. Just remember to play it safe, stay vigilant, and savor every moment out on the open water.

As we wrap up Chapter 2, it's clear that identifying fish and understanding their habitats is essential for any angler. From recognizing different species to deciphering their behaviors and preferred environments, we've covered a lot of ground. Armed with this knowledge, you're better equipped to read the aquatic landscape like a seasoned angler. Remember, fishing is as much about observation and adaptation as it is about technique and skill. Whether you're casting lines in rivers, lakes, or oceans, keep exploring, keep learning, and most importantly, keep enjoying the thrill of the chase.

Chapter 3:

Fly Fishing

Picture this: You're standing knee-deep in a mountain stream, the early morning mist swirling around you like a scene from a dream. In one hand, you hold a meticulously crafted fly rod, while in the other, a line dances gracefully through the air, propelled by the rhythmic flick of your wrist. Ahead lies the promise of elusive trout, their silvery forms darting beneath the crystal-clear waters. This, my friend, is the enchanting world of fly fishing.

Fly fishing isn't just about catching fish—it's an experience that immerses you in nature's embrace. It's about the delicate dance of an artificial fly upon the water's surface, enticing even the wariest of fish to rise and strike. It's about the camaraderie between angler and the environment, where each cast becomes a meditation, and each catch a triumph.

But fly fishing isn't all serious business—there's plenty of room for laughter and lightheartedness along the way. After all, anyone who's ever tangled their line in a tree or mistaken their own hat for a trout knows that fly fishing comes with its fair share of comedic moments. So, as we embark on this journey into the art of fly fishing, let's keep our spirits high and our lines tight.

Whether you're a seasoned angler or a curious novice, this chapter promises to unravel the secrets of fly fishing in all its elegance and finesse. From understanding the intricacies of fly selection to mastering the art of casting, we'll explore every facet of this timeless pursuit.

The Fly Fishing Experience

Fly fishing isn't just about catching fish—it's a holistic pursuit that intertwines the angler, the fly, and the environment into a harmonious dance.

Fly Fishing as a Holistic Pursuit

Unlike other forms of fishing that may prioritize the catch above all else, fly fishing places equal emphasis on the experience itself. It's about immersing yourself in nature, connecting with the rhythm of the river, and finding solace in the serenity of the outdoors. From the tranquil beauty of mountain streams to the vast expanse of coastal flats, every fly fishing adventure offers a chance to escape the hustle and bustle of daily life and reconnect with the natural world.

The Angler, the Fly, and the Environment

At the heart of fly fishing lies the dynamic interplay between the angler, the fly, and the environment. As the angler stands amid the rushing currents or serene still waters, they become an integral part of the ecosystem, attuned to the nuances of the river or lake. Each cast is a delicate ballet, with the fly serving as a vessel for communication between angler and fish. Whether it's the gentle flutter of a dry fly on the surface or the rhythmic pulsing of a streamer through deeper waters, every movement is infused with intention and purpose.

Rhythmic Casting and Anticipation

One of the most captivating aspects of fly fishing is the rhythmic casting of the fly line, a mesmerizing dance that requires both skill and finesse. With each cast, the angler weaves a tapestry of motion, sending the fly sailing through the air with precision and grace. There's a meditative quality to casting, a sense of mindfulness that comes from focusing solely on the movement of line and fly. As the line unfurls in a graceful arc, anticipation builds with each twitch and drift, culminating in the electrifying moment when a trout rises to take the bait.

In essence, the fly fishing experience transcends the act of catching fish—it's about forging a deep connection with the natural world and finding joy in the simple act of casting a line.

Philosophy of the Sport

In the realm of fly fishing, there's a rich philosophy that guides every angler on their quest for the perfect catch. Central to this philosophy is the understanding of the fly—a delicate concoction of feathers, fur, and thread that seeks to mimic the insects and aquatic creatures that inhabit a fish's diet.

Understanding the Fly

Alright, so let's dive a bit deeper into understanding the fly in fly fishing. At its very core, fly fishing is all about the art of fly tying. It's this centuries-old tradition where anglers transform these really humble materials into these intricate imitations of nature's bounty. I mean, we're talking about everything from delicate dry flies that kind of dance upon the water's surface to these weighted nymphs that just drift along the riverbed.

Each fly is crafted with this incredible attention to detail and precision because, you know what, fish are smart! They're not easily fooled. So, when we're out there on the water, we're essentially presenting these flies to the fish as if they were the real deal, like a natural insect or baitfish. It's all about creating that illusion, that deception, to entice even the most discerning of fish to strike. And let me tell you, when it works, there's nothing quite like it!

The Art of Fly Tying

Picture this: You're sitting at your fly-tying bench, surrounded by an array of colorful feathers, fur patches, and spools of thread. With each delicate motion of your fingers, you bring to life a miniature masterpiece—a fly that not only looks like the real deal but also has the potential to fool even the most cautious of fish.

Fly tying is like painting with nature's palette, where every material has its place and purpose. Whether you're crafting a dainty dry fly to imitate a delicate mayfly or sculpting a bulky streamer to mimic a fleeing minnow, each pattern is a work of art in its own right. And the best part? You're not just copying nature; you're interpreting it through your own creative lens.

But it's not just about aesthetics—it's about functionality, too. The materials you choose and the techniques you employ can greatly influence how your fly behaves in the water. A well-tied fly should not only look good but also move convincingly, enticing fish to strike with each tantalizing twitch.

So, as you sit down at your fly-tying bench, remember that you're not just tying flies—you're creating a connection between angler and fish, between art and nature. And with each fly you tie, you're adding another chapter to the rich tapestry of fly fishing lore.

Selecting the Right Fly Patterns

Suppose you are standing by a beautiful river, the sun gently warming your back as you prepare to cast your line. Now, imagine that you're faced with a vast array of flies, each one promising to entice that elusive trout lurking beneath the surface. How do you choose the right one?

First things first, consider the time of year. Different seasons bring different insect hatches, and trout tend to feed on what's abundant at the moment. For example, in the spring, you might encounter mayfly hatches, while in summer, you could bring caddisflies or stoneflies. By knowing what insects are prevalent during each season, you can select flies that closely resemble the natural prey.

Next, take a look at the prevailing weather conditions. Is it sunny and warm, or overcast and rainy? Weather can significantly impact insect activity and fish behavior. On bright days, trout may be more cautious and selective in their feeding, so you might opt for smaller, more subtle patterns. On the other hand, cloudy days might trigger more aggressive feeding behavior, allowing you to use larger, more visible flies.

Now, let's talk about the specific species of fish you're targeting. Different fish have different feeding preferences, so it's essential to choose flies that appeal to their tastes. For example, if you're going after trout, you'll want to use patterns that mimic the insects and other aquatic creatures they commonly feed on. If you're targeting bass or panfish, you might opt for larger, more brightly colored flies that elicit a predatory response.

Matching the Hatch

Now, let's talk about one of the most important concepts in fly fishing: matching the hatch. Let's say you're standing knee-deep in a crystal-clear river, the sun gently warming your back as you scan the water's surface for any signs of activity. Suddenly, you notice a flurry of insect activity—a mayfly hatch is underway, and the trout are rising to feast. This is where matching the hatch comes into play.

Matching the hatch is all about presenting flies that closely resemble the insects and aquatic creatures that fish are actively feeding on. It's like putting the perfect dish in front of a hungry diner—it's irresistible.

But how do you know what the fish are eating? Well, that's where observation comes in.

By carefully watching the water's surface, you can identify the insects in their various life stages. Are they tiny midges dancing on the surface, or perhaps larger mayflies gently floating downstream? Once you've identified the main course, it's time to pick the right fly from your box.

You want your fly to mimic not just the size and shape of the natural prey, but also its color. After all, trout can be picky eaters, and they won't hesitate to turn up their noses at something that doesn't look quite right. So, whether it's a delicate mayfly hatch on a warm summer evening or a frenzied caddis emergence in the early morning hours, matching the hatch is your ticket to success on the water.

Think of it as speaking the fish's language. When you present them with a fly that looks and behaves like their favorite snack, they're much more likely to take the bait. So, the next time you're out on the river, pay close attention to what's happening around you, and don't be afraid to switch up your fly selection to match the hatch. Trust me, the fish will thank you for it.

In essence, the philosophy of fly fishing is grounded in a deep respect for the natural world and a profound appreciation for the artistry and craftsmanship that define the sport.

Casting as an Art Form

Alright, let's move on to casting—a fundamental aspect of fly fishing that can be both a challenge and a pleasure. Picture yourself standing on the bank of a serene river, the sun glinting off the water as you prepare to make your first cast. It's a moment of anticipation, excitement, and maybe a little bit of nerves. But fear not, because we're about to dive into the delicate art of casting.

First off, let's talk about the importance of delicate and precise casting. In fly fishing, it's all about finesse. Unlike traditional bait or lure fishing, where you might simply cast out and let the weight of your gear do the work, fly fishing demands a different approach. Think of it like this: You're not just tossing a weighted hook into the water—you're delicately presenting a tiny, lightweight fly that's meant to mimic the insects or aquatic creatures that fish love to eat.

Now, imagine that delicate fly is attached to a thin leader and tippet—a fine, almost invisible thread that connects your fly to your line. Every movement you make, from the flick of your wrist to the angle of your cast, has to be precise. There's no room for error here. If your cast is too harsh, your fly might smack down on the water's surface like a lead weight, scaring off any nearby fish. But if it's too gentle, your fly might not land where you want it to, missing out on that perfect spot where the big ones are lurking.

That's the beauty of fly fishing—it's a delicate dance between angler and fish, where every movement counts. It's like trying to thread a needle with a feather in a gentle breeze. It takes skill, patience, and a whole lot of practice. But when you get it just right—when your cast lands softly on the water's surface, exactly where you wanted it to—that's when the magic happens. That's when the fish rise up to take your fly, and you feel that thrill of the chase that keeps anglers coming back for more. So next time you're out on the water, remember: *In fly fishing, precision is key*.

Now, when it comes to casting techniques, there are a few different approaches you can take.

Overhead Cast

One of the most common is the overhead cast. When it comes to casting techniques in fly fishing, the overhead cast reigns supreme as one of the most fundamental and widely used methods. Let's say you are standing on the bank of a tranquil river, with the gentle flow of water beckoning you to cast your line. As you raise your rod tip skyward, you're preparing to execute the elegant overhead cast—a maneuver that's as timeless as it is effective.

With the overhead cast, you begin by smoothly raising the rod tip behind you, allowing the line to unfurl gracefully behind you like a dancer stretching before a performance. As you reach the apex of your backcast, you pause for just a moment, feeling the weight of the line load the rod tip with potential energy.

Then, with a flick of your wrist and a subtle forward motion, you release that pent-up energy, sending the line shooting forward with precision and grace. The line whistles through the air like a silk ribbon, landing softly on the water's surface with a gentle plop.

The overhead cast is a versatile technique that's perfect for covering short to medium distances with pinpoint accuracy. Whether you're casting to rising trout in a narrow stream or presenting a fly to cruising bonefish on a saltwater flat, the overhead cast gives you the control and finesse you need to make those critical presentations.

Double Haul

But what about when you need to cast a bit farther or deal with tricky wind conditions? That's where the double haul comes in. Suppose you've spotted a school of bonefish cruising just out of reach, but the wind is howling and your standard casting technique just isn't cutting it. You need the double haul.

So, what exactly is the double haul? Well, it's a casting technique that involves using both hands to generate extra power and speed on your forward cast. Here's how it works: As you bring the rod back behind you on your backcast, you simultaneously pull down on the line with your line hand while pushing up with your rod hand. This creates tension in the line, loading the rod with energy like a coiled spring.

Then, as you make your forward cast, you release the tension in the line with a quick, sharp pull of your line hand while simultaneously accelerating the rod forward with your rod hand. This sudden burst of energy propels the line forward with incredible speed and accuracy, allowing you to punch through the wind and reach those distant fish with ease.

Now, I won't lie to you—the double haul is a bit tricky to master at first. It requires precise timing, coordination, and a good bit of practice. But trust me when I say that once you get the hang of it, you'll wonder how you ever fished without it. Suddenly, those windy days and distant targets won't seem so daunting anymore.

Dry Fly Presentation vs. Double Haul

Now, let's talk about the age-old debate: dry fly presentation vs. double haul. Dry fly presentation is all about delicacy and finesse, while the double haul is more about power and distance. Which one is right for you? Well, that depends on the situation.

If you're fishing a calm, glassy pool on a sunny day and you want to present your fly with the utmost delicacy, then dry fly presentation is the way to go. It's like laying down a feather on the water—soft, subtle, and oh-so-effective. But if you're dealing with a stiff breeze or you need to reach a distant target, then the double haul is your best friend. With its extra power and speed, it's like launching a missile at your target—fast, efficient, and deadly accurate.

So, whether you're casting a dry fly to rising trout on a tranquil mountain stream or double hauling your way to a distant school of bonefish on a windy saltwater flat, mastering the delicate art of casting is sure to take your fly fishing game to new heights.

Reading the Water for Fly Fishing

Let's dive into the art of reading the water for fly fishing, where every ripple, eddy, and current tells a story waiting to be deciphered.

Deciphering the Currents

As you gaze out at the water's surface, it's like peering into a living tapestry of currents, each telling its own story. To the untrained eye, it may seem like a chaotic swirl of motion, but to the seasoned angler, it's a treasure trove of information waiting to be decoded.

Deciphering the currents is like unraveling a mystery, where every eddy, riffle, and seam holds clues to the whereabouts of the elusive trout. Start by observing the surface of the water, where subtle nuances reveal hidden secrets. Look for seams—those invisible lines where fast-moving currents meet slower flows, creating a natural highway for insects and food sources. These seams are like bustling thoroughfares for hungry trout, offering easy access to a smorgasbord of delectable treats.

Position yourself strategically upstream of these seams, where the current carries your fly naturally into the feeding zone. With a deft flick of your wrist, send your fly dancing across the surface, mimicking the delicate movements of a hapless insect. Watch as it drifts effortlessly downstream, tantalizingly close to the waiting jaws of hungry trout.

But decoding the currents isn't just about finding feeding lanes—it's also about understanding the behavior of the fish. Trout are opportunistic feeders, lurking in the shadows of submerged rocks and fallen branches, waiting for the perfect moment to strike. By reading the currents, you can anticipate their movements and present your fly with precision and accuracy.

Identifying Feeding Lanes

Identifying feeding lanes is like discovering the hidden gems of a river—the secret spots where fish gather to indulge in their favorite treats. Picture it like this: You're strolling through a bustling marketplace, and suddenly, you spot a crowd gathered around a street food vendor. That's your cue to investigate because where there's a crowd, there's bound to be something tasty on offer.

Similarly, on the water's surface, keep an eye out for any signs of activity that suggest fish are on the hunt. Look for subtle disturbances like dimples, swirls, or the occasional flash of silver as fish dart beneath the surface. These are the telltale signs of feeding lanes, where fish congregate to feed on insects, baitfish, or other delectable morsels.

Once you've pinpointed a feeding lane, it's time to make your move. Position yourself upstream of the action, so your fly drifts naturally into the feeding zone, just like a delectable appetizer wafting past a hungry diner's nose. Take care to mend your line to avoid any drag that might spook the fish, and then, with a flick of the wrist, let your fly dance enticingly on the water's surface.

Now, it's a waiting game—a test of patience and skill as you watch with bated breath for that unmistakable tug on the line. And when it comes, oh, what a thrill! The adrenaline rush as the fish takes the bait, the adrenaline-fueled battle as you reel it in—it's pure angling bliss, all thanks to the art of identifying feeding lanes.

Understanding Water Flow

Understanding water flow is like deciphering the language of the river—a skill that separates the novice angler from the seasoned pro. It's not just about knowing where to cast your fly—it's about understanding the rhythm and pulse of the river itself.

When you step into the water, take a moment to observe the surface. Look for the subtle clues that reveal the river's secrets. Riffles, those shimmering stretches of water where the surface seems to dance with energy, are like bustling city streets bustling with life. Insects dart and dance in the currents, providing a smorgasbord for hungry trout.

But don't overlook the quieter spots—the runs and pools that offer respite from the frenetic pace of the riffles. Runs are the steady, reliable arteries of the river, where fish seek refuge from the swift currents and find sanctuary in the deeper water. Pools, on the other hand, are the tranquil oases where fish gather to rest and feed. They're like cozy living rooms, inviting trout to kick back and relax in the cool, calm waters.

Understanding water flow isn't just about knowing where the fish are—it's about anticipating their next move. It's about recognizing the subtle shifts in current speed and direction that signal a change in feeding behavior. It's about knowing when to present your fly with a delicate touch and when to unleash the power of the double haul.

So, the next time you find yourself on the river, take a moment to tune in to the language of the water. Listen to its whispers and watch its movements. And remember, when you understand water flow, you hold the key to unlocking the secrets of the river and the fish that call it home.

Presentation and Drift Control

Achieving a natural drift is the holy grail of fly fishing—it's what separates the amateurs from the pros. But mastering the art of presentation and drift control isn't just about luck; it's about understanding the subtle nuances of the river and knowing how to work with them to your advantage.

Achieving a Natural Drift

Achieving a natural drift is the essence of fly fishing finesse. It's about creating an illusion so convincing that even the most discerning trout can't resist. Imagine you're a fish, cruising along in the current, minding your own business when suddenly you spot something that looks too good to be true—a tasty morsel drifting effortlessly downstream. That's the moment you've been waiting for.

But here's the thing—fish aren't easily fooled. They've seen it all before, and they know the difference between a convincing imitation and a clumsy impostor. That's where achieving a natural drift comes in. It's about making your fly behave as if it belongs in the river, blending seamlessly into the aquatic landscape like a master of disguise.

So, how do you pull off this feat of angling artistry? It starts with careful observation and attention to detail. You need to study the water's surface, paying close attention to the speed and direction of the current. Look for subtle eddies, seams, and foam lines that indicate where fish are likely to hold. Then, adjust your casting angle and presentation to match the natural flow of the river, so your fly drifts downstream in a lifelike manner.

But achieving a natural drift isn't just about technical skill—it's also about instinct and intuition. It's about learning to read the river like a book, anticipating where fish will be lying in wait and positioning your fly accordingly. It's about feeling the rhythm of the water in your bones and responding with subtle adjustments to keep your fly in the strike zone.

Ultimately, achieving a natural drift is a delicate dance between angler and river, a symbiotic relationship built on trust and mutual respect. It's about surrendering control and allowing the current to guide you, trusting in the wisdom of the water to lead you to success.

Subtleties of Presentation

Mastering the subtleties of presentation is like learning to speak the language of the river fluently. It's not just about making a cast; it's about making the right cast at the right time, in the right way. Picture yourself as a conductor, guiding your fly through a symphony of currents with grace and precision.

First, let's talk about controlling the speed of your cast. Think of it like Goldilocks and the Three Bears—not too fast, not too slow, but just right. You want your fly to land on the water with a soft touch, like a feather drifting down from the sky. Too much speed and it'll splash down like a cannonball, scaring away every fish in the vicinity. Too little speed and it'll plop down like a lead weight, sinking before it has a chance to entice a strike. Finding that perfect balance takes practice, but once you do, you'll be amazed at how many more fish start taking notice.

Next, let's talk about the angle of your cast. This is where things get really interesting. Depending on the layout of the river and the behavior of the fish, you may need to adjust the angle of your cast to achieve the desired presentation. Sometimes that means casting upstream and letting your fly drift downstream naturally with the current. Other times it means casting across the current and using mends to control the drift. And sometimes it means casting downstream and skating your fly across the surface like a fleeing insect. Each approach has its own unique challenges and rewards, but the key is to stay adaptable and open to new possibilities.

Finally, let's talk about finesse and precision. These are the secret ingredients that separate the good anglers from the great ones. It's not just about making a cast—it's about making the perfect cast, every time. That means hitting your target with pinpoint accuracy, landing your fly with a gentle touch, and controlling the drift with subtle adjustments. It's like threading a needle in a hurricane—difficult, but not impossible. With practice and perseverance, you'll soon find yourself casting with the grace and precision of a seasoned pro and reaping the rewards in the form of more fish in the net.

Mending Line and Controlling Drift

But presentation is just the beginning. Once your fly hits the water, you need to be prepared to make adjustments on the fly (pun intended). That's where mending line and controlling drift come into play. Mending line is like playing tug-of-war with the current, using subtle movements of your rod and line to adjust the speed and direction of your drift. It's a skill that takes time to master, but once you get the hang of it, you'll wonder how you ever fished without it.

Controlling drift is all about staying one step ahead of the river. It's about anticipating how the current will affect your fly and making split-second decisions to keep it on course. Sometimes, that means feeding out line to slow down your drift, and other times, it means lifting your rod tip to speed it up. It's a delicate balancing act that requires patience, practice, and a keen understanding of the river's rhythms.

So, the next time you find yourself on the water, remember: Achieving a natural drift isn't just about luck—it's about mastering the art of presentation and drift control.

Mountain Streams and Creeks

The serenity of mountain streams and creeks—the perfect playground for fly fishing enthusiasts seeking a more intimate and challenging experience. In these narrow waterways, stealth and precision are your allies as you navigate the rugged terrain in pursuit of native trout.

Stealth and Precision

In the world of mountain streams and creeks, stealth and precision are not just optional—they're essential skills for any angler hoping to reel in those elusive trout. Picture yourself as a stealthy ninja, silently gliding along the rocky banks, your every move calculated to avoid detection. The fish may be wary, but with the right approach, you can outsmart even the most cautious trout.

Stealth is your first line of defense in these tight quarters, where the fish are easily spooked by the slightest disturbance. That's why it's essential to move with the grace and subtlety of a ballet dancer, taking care to avoid sudden movements and loud noises. Camouflage clothing helps you blend seamlessly into your surroundings, while low-profile casts minimize your impact on the water. It's all about becoming one with the river, blending into the background so that the fish never even know you're there.

But stealth alone won't guarantee success—you also need precision. With obstacles lurking around every bend and tight casting quarters to contend with, you'll need to be able to place your fly with pinpoint accuracy. Every cast is a delicate dance, a careful calculation of angles and trajectories designed to deliver your fly to the most promising lies. It's a game of inches, where one false move can send your fly drifting hopelessly off course.

So, as you navigate the rocky banks and crystal-clear waters of mountain streams and creeks, remember the importance of stealth and precision. Blend into your surroundings like a ghost, moving with the grace and subtlety of a natural-born angler. And when it comes time to make your cast, do so with confidence and precision, knowing that each movement brings you one step closer to that elusive trout.

Pursuing Native Trout

Pursuing native trout in mountain streams and creeks is a thrilling adventure that every fly angler dreams of. Here's why it's so exhilarating:

- **Wild and elusive:** Native trout are the epitome of wildness, with their vibrant colors and elusive nature adding an air of mystery to every encounter. Their feisty attitudes and lightning-fast reflexes make them a challenging adversary for even the most seasoned anglers.

- **Legendary status:** Native trout hold a special place in the hearts of anglers worldwide, their reputation as the ultimate prize fish only adding to their allure. From the majestic rainbow trout to the elusive brook trout, each species carries its own mystique and charm.

- **Skill and patience:** Catching native trout is no easy feat—it requires a combination of skill, patience, and a deep understanding of their habitat and behavior. From reading the water to presenting your fly with precision, every aspect of the angling experience must be carefully orchestrated to outsmart these cunning fish.

- **Habitat and behavior:** Native trout are intimately connected to their environment, with their behavior dictated by the unique characteristics of mountain streams and creeks. Understanding where they hide, what they eat, and how they react to changes in their surroundings is key to unlocking their secrets.

- **Natural beauty:** Perhaps the greatest reward of pursuing native trout is the opportunity to immerse yourself in the breathtaking beauty of their natural habitat. From crystal-clear mountain streams to lush, moss-covered banks, every moment spent on the water is a feast for the senses.

In the end, pursuing native trout is about more than just catching fish—it's about embracing the thrill of the chase, the beauty of the natural world, and the joy of immersing yourself in the timeless art of fly fishing.

Challenges and Rewards

Navigating the treacherous terrain of mountain streams and creeks is like embarking on a rugged wilderness expedition. As you traverse rocky banks, ford babbling brooks, and scramble over fallen logs, each step presents a new challenge and a test of your outdoor prowess. But amidst the obstacles and obstacles lies the promise of untold treasures—the chance to encounter some of nature's most elusive and captivating creatures.

Outsmarting wily trout in these remote waters requires more than just luck—it demands cunning, patience, and a keen understanding of fish behavior. These native trout have honed their survival instincts over generations, making them some of the most challenging adversaries an angler can face. But with perseverance and a bit of ingenuity, you can unlock the secrets of their habitat and tempt them into striking your fly.

And when that magical moment finally arrives—when you feel the unmistakable tug on your line and see a shimmering trout dancing on the end of your rod—all the challenges and obstacles fade away in an instant. In that fleeting moment, you're transported to a world of pure exhilaration and triumph, where the thrill of the catch eclipses all else.

It's moments like these that make mountain stream fishing so rewarding. It's not just about the fish you catch or the miles you trek—it's about the memories you make and the connections you forge with the natural world. So, as you set off on your next adventure in the mountains, remember to savor every challenge and embrace every reward, for in the end, it's all part of the timeless allure of fly fishing.

Stillwater Fly Fishing

Fly fishing in lakes and ponds presents anglers with a unique canvas for exploration. Unlike the ever-changing currents of rivers and streams, the calm and often serene waters of lakes and ponds offer a different kind of angling experience. Here, anglers are not just casting into the flow but rather into vast expanses of stillness, where every movement of the fly is magnified, and every subtle change in presentation can make a difference.

When you step onto the shores of a lake or pond, you enter a world of tranquility and possibility. The stillness of the water reflects the surrounding landscape like a mirror, inviting you to cast your line and explore its depths. Whether you choose to wade along the shoreline or drift quietly in a boat, the art of stillwater fly fishing demands a unique set of skills and techniques.

Patience is paramount in stillwater fly fishing, as success often requires waiting for the perfect moment to present your fly. Unlike the fast-paced action of river fishing, where trout are constantly on the move, stillwater trout tend to be more selective and deliberate in their feeding habits. As an angler, you must be prepared to observe and wait for the subtle signs that indicate the presence of feeding fish, such as rising trout or the occasional splash of a feeding fish.

Observation is also key in stillwater fly fishing, as understanding the behavior of trout in lakes and ponds requires keen powers of observation. By carefully watching the water's surface for signs of insect activity or fish movement, anglers can gain valuable insights into where trout are likely to be holding and what they may be feeding on. This knowledge allows anglers to make informed decisions about fly selection, presentation, and strategy.

Strategic thinking is essential for success in stillwater fly fishing, as anglers must constantly adapt their tactics to the changing conditions of the lake or pond. Factors such as wind direction, water temperature, and time of day can all influence fish behavior and feeding patterns, requiring anglers to adjust their approach accordingly. Whether it's selecting the right fly pattern, adjusting your casting angle, or varying your retrieve speed, strategic thinking is essential for consistently fooling wary trout in still waters.

In essence, mastering the art of stillwater fly fishing is about embracing the unique challenges and rewards that come with fishing in lakes and ponds. It's about learning to read the water, understand fish behavior, and adapt your tactics to the ever-changing conditions of the environment.

Strategies for Enticing Cruising Trout

Understanding the behavior of cruising trout is paramount in stillwater fly fishing. These trout, unlike those in rivers, wander the open waters of lakes and ponds, constantly on the lookout for their next meal. To entice these elusive fish, anglers must employ strategic tactics that mimic the natural movements of their prey.

One effective strategy is to use imitative fly patterns that closely resemble the aquatic insects and small baitfish that trout feed on. For example, nymph patterns can imitate the immature stages of aquatic insects, while streamers can mimic small fish or other prey items. By selecting flies that match the size, shape, and color of the natural forage in the water, anglers increase their chances of enticing cruising trout to strike.

In addition to fly selection, presentation plays a crucial role in enticing cruising trout. Anglers must consider factors such as depth, retrieve speed, and movement to make their flies appear as natural and appealing as possible. This may involve using a variety of retrieval techniques, such as slow retrieves to imitate injured prey or erratic retrieves to mimic fleeing baitfish. Experimenting with different presentations can help anglers determine what triggers a response from cruising trout on any given day.

Furthermore, anglers should pay close attention to the behavior of cruising trout and adjust their tactics accordingly. For example, if trout are actively feeding near the surface, dry fly or emerger patterns may be the most effective choice. On the other hand, if trout are holding deeper in the water column, sinking lines and weighted flies may be necessary to reach them.

Adapting to Open Waters

Adapting to open waters in stillwater fly fishing is like navigating a vast expanse of uncharted territory. Unlike the confined channels of rivers and streams, lakes and ponds present anglers with expansive, featureless landscapes where fish could be lurking anywhere. To conquer these open waters, anglers must employ a variety of techniques and strategies tailored to the unique challenges of stillwater fly fishing.

One key tactic for adapting to open waters is trolling, a method where anglers slowly motor or paddle a boat while trailing their flies behind them. Trolling allows anglers to cover large areas of water efficiently, presenting their flies to a wide range of depths and locations where fish might be holding. By varying the speed and depth of their presentation, anglers can systematically search for productive fishing spots and increase their chances of success.

Another effective technique for adapting to open waters is prospecting, which involves casting and retrieving flies across different areas of the lake or pond in search of actively feeding fish. This method requires anglers to remain mobile and flexible, constantly scanning the water for signs of fish activity such as rises, swirls, or surface disturbances. By moving from spot to spot and experimenting with different fly patterns and retrieves, anglers can increase their chances of encountering feeding trout and other gamefish.

In addition to trolling and prospecting, successful anglers must also pay close attention to environmental factors such as wind direction, water temperature, and light conditions. These variables can have a significant impact on fish behavior and feeding patterns, so anglers must be prepared to adjust their tactics accordingly. For example, on windy days, trout may be more active near the surface where food is blown by the wind, while on calm days, they may retreat to deeper water where they feel safer from predators.

Ultimately, stillwater fly fishing offers anglers a unique and rewarding angling experience. Whether you're casting to rising trout from the shoreline or drifting across a tranquil pond in a boat, the challenges and opportunities presented by still waters are bound to keep you coming back for more.

Saltwater Fly Fishing

Saltwater fly fishing opens up a whole new world of angling adventures, where the salty air and crashing waves provide the backdrop for thrilling encounters with some of the ocean's most prized species. From stalking bonefish on tropical flats to battling monster tarpon in coastal estuaries, saltwater fly fishing offers anglers a chance to test their skills against some of the most powerful and elusive fish in the sea. However, navigating the dynamic environment of the saltwater realm requires a different approach than freshwater fly fishing, as anglers must contend with shifting tides, unpredictable currents, and a host of other factors that can make or break a day on the water.

Extending Fly Fishing to Coastal Flats

Extending fly fishing to coastal flats is like stepping into a whole new realm of adventure. Imagine yourself standing amid the serene beauty of shallow, sandy expanses, with nothing but the gentle lapping of waves and the occasional cry of seabirds to break the silence. The water around you is so clear you can see straight to the bottom, where schools of bonefish, permit, and other flats species glide gracefully in search of their next meal.

Here, every movement must be deliberate and calculated. Anglers wade quietly through the water, their eyes scanning the flats for any sign of movement—a flick of a tail, a glimmer of silver, the subtle disturbance of the water. It's a game of patience and observation, where success hinges on your ability to spot the elusive targets and make your move at just the right moment.

And when that moment comes, when you finally spot a tailing bonefish or a cruising permit, the adrenaline starts pumping and your heart starts racing. It's the thrill of the hunt, the excitement of the chase, and the anticipation of what's to come. You carefully strip out line, making sure to keep it taut and ready for action. Your fly lands with a delicate plop, and you hold your breath, waiting for the fish to make its move.

And then it happens—the water explodes as the fish lunges for your fly, its tail thrashing wildly as it tries to shake the hook. You set the hook with a quick flick of your wrist, and suddenly you're locked in a battle of wills with one of the ocean's most prized inhabitants. It's a tug-of-war unlike any other, with the fish testing your strength, skill, and patience to the limit.

But for all the challenges it presents, saltwater fly fishing on the coastal flats is also incredibly rewarding. There's nothing quite like the feeling of landing that first bonefish or permit, of holding it in your hands and marveling at its beauty. It's a moment of triumph, a validation of all your hard work and dedication.

Encounter With Saltwater Species

Each species presents its own unique set of challenges and opportunities, requiring anglers to adapt their tactics and techniques accordingly. Take tarpon, for example. These silver kings are known for their aerial displays and blistering runs, making them one of the most sought-after species in saltwater fly fishing. To hook into a tarpon is to engage in a battle of strength and wits, with the outcome hanging in the balance with every surge and leap.

Or consider sailfish, with their distinctive dorsal fins and lightning-fast strikes. Targeting these majestic creatures requires patience, skill, and a keen eye for spotting their telltale signs—a dorsal fin cutting through the water, a flash of silver beneath the surface. And once you've hooked into a sailfish, be prepared for an adrenaline-fueled fight that will test your tackle and your resolve to the limit.

But it's not just about the big game species. Saltwater fly fishing offers opportunities to target a wide variety of fish, from the feisty stripers and bluefish that patrol the coastal waters to the elusive bonefish and permit that haunt the shallow flats. Whether you're casting poppers to surface-feeding stripers or stripping streamers through a school of marauding bluefish, saltwater fly fishing offers endless opportunities for excitement and adventure.

And let's not forget about the thrill of the chase. Whether you're stalking bonefish on the flats or hunting marlin in the open ocean, there's nothing quite like the adrenaline rush of seeing your target, making the cast, and watching as the fish homes in on your fly. It's a moment of pure exhilaration, a fleeting glimpse of the wildness and beauty that lies beneath the surface of the sea.

Adapting to Tides and Currents

Navigating the ebb and flow of tides and currents is like trying to solve a puzzle with pieces that are constantly shifting. In saltwater fly fishing, mastering this puzzle is essential for success, but it's no easy feat. Imagine standing on the shore, watching as the water rises and falls with the rhythm of the tides. With each passing hour, the currents shift and swirl, carrying with them the promise of hungry fish and the challenge of unpredictable conditions.

To thrive in this ever-changing environment, anglers must become masters of adaptation. They must learn to anticipate the movements of the tides and plan their fishing trips accordingly, choosing the optimal times to target feeding fish and avoiding periods of slack water when fish are less active.

But adapting to tides and currents goes beyond simply timing your fishing trips. It's also about understanding how these forces shape the underwater landscape and influence fish behavior. For example, strong currents can create underwater highways that fish use to travel between feeding and resting areas, while tidal flows can concentrate baitfish and other prey, drawing predators in their wake.

To capitalize on these opportunities, anglers must learn to read the water like a book, deciphering the subtle clues that reveal the presence of fish and the paths they're likely to follow. They must position themselves strategically, casting their flies into the path of oncoming fish and using the natural flow of the current to their advantage.

But perhaps the greatest challenge of all is learning to adapt on the fly. In saltwater fly fishing, conditions can change in an instant, turning calm seas into roiling waves and gentle currents into raging torrents. To succeed in this dynamic environment, anglers must be flexible and responsive, adjusting their tactics and techniques to suit the ever-changing conditions.

So, if you're ready to take on the challenge of saltwater fly fishing, be prepared to adapt and evolve with the tides. Embrace the unpredictability of the sea, and you'll discover a world of excitement and adventure waiting just beneath the surface.

As we come to the end of this chapter, it's clear that fly fishing is more than just a sport—it's a way of life. From the gentle rhythm of casting a fly line to the thrill of hooking into a feisty trout, every moment on the water is an opportunity for adventure and discovery.

We've explored the art of fly tying, the nuances of casting, and the secrets of reading the water. We've delved into mountain streams, stillwater lakes, and saltwater flats, uncovering the unique challenges and rewards of each environment.

But beyond the technical skills and strategies, fly fishing is ultimately about connection—connection to the natural world, to the fish we pursue, and to ourselves. It's a chance to slow down, unplug, and immerse ourselves in the beauty and wonder of the great outdoors.

Whether you're a seasoned angler or a complete beginner, I hope this chapter has inspired you to pick up a fly rod and experience the magic of fly fishing for yourself. Remember, the journey is just beginning, and the possibilities are endless.

Chapter 4:

Fish Preparation, Filleting, and Steaking

In this chapter, we will begin a journey from the water to the table, turning the day's catch into delectable delights. We will dive deep into the art of fish filleting, a skill that transforms fish into culinary masterpieces. But before we get started, let's make sure we're properly equipped. Picture this: you, a sharp fillet knife, and a clean workspace—a trio destined for fish filleting greatness. Oh, and don't forget your nonslip cutting board—because the last thing you want is your fish slipping away like a slippery fish from your grasp!

Now, let's talk safety. We're not defusing bombs here, but proper knife-handling techniques are crucial. Think of it as a dance—a delicate, coordinated dance between you and your knife. So, grab your fillet knife with confidence, but treat it with respect. After all, we're here to fillet fish, not fingers!

Once we've got our tools and safety measures sorted, it's time to dive into the nitty-gritty of fish preparation. Scaling the fish is our first order of business. We want a clean canvas, free from those pesky scales that stick to everything like tiny fishy confetti. And trust me, nobody wants a mouthful of fish scales—unless you're auditioning for a role in *The Little Mermaid*, of course!

Next up, gutting the fish—because nobody likes a fishy surprise. We're talking swift and efficient gutting here, like a well-oiled machine. Think of it as an operation—precision is key! With our fish scaled and gutted, we're ready to tackle the main event: filleting and steaking. It's time to unleash your inner sushi chef and turn that fish into boneless fillets or succulent steaks.

But wait, there's more! Pin-bone removal, portion control, and even culinary sustainability—because we're not just filleting fish, we're saving the planet, one fish scrap at a time. So, buckle up, grab your fillet knife, and let's dive into the wonderful world of fish preparation!

Gearing Up

Alright, folks, let's get down to business! Before we start slicing and dicing our catch of the day, we need to make sure we're properly equipped. Think of it like gearing up for battle—except instead of swords and shields, we're armed with fillet knives and cutting boards. So, let's take inventory of our arsenal and make sure we've got everything we need to conquer the filleting frontier!

Essential Tools for Fish Cleaning, Filleting, and Steaking

First things first, let's talk tools. You wouldn't bring a spoon to a knife fight, right? Well, the same goes for fish filleting. So, without further ado, here's a closer look at what you'll need:

- **Fillet knife:** Ah, the fillet knife—the unsung hero of every angler's toolkit. This bad boy is your ticket to slicing and dicing with surgical precision. But not just any knife will do! You need one with a sharp, flexible blade that can glide effortlessly through fish flesh. Remember, a dull knife is like trying to cut through a brick wall with a feather duster—ineffective and downright frustrating.

- **Cutting surface:** Now, let's talk about where all the action happens—the cutting surface. You wouldn't want your prized catch slipping and sliding around like a fish out of water, would you? That's where a sturdy cutting board comes into play. Opt for one that's stable and preferably nonslip to prevent any accidental seafood aerobatics. Trust me, trying to corral a slippery fish on a wobbly surface is a recipe for disaster!

- **Clean workspace:** Last but certainly not least, you need a clean workspace to work your filleting magic. I'm talking about clearing off your kitchen counter and creating a pristine, dedicated space for your fish filleting endeavors. Nobody wants to discover a stray fish scale in their morning cereal, right? So, grab a sponge, roll up your sleeves, and get ready to transform your kitchen into a filleting sanctuary.

With your fillet knife sharpened, your cutting surface secured, and your workspace sparkling clean, you're ready to tackle the next step in the fish filleting process.

Importance of a Sharp Fillet Knife and Clean Workspace

Let's dive a bit deeper into why a sharp fillet knife and a clean workspace are absolutely crucial for successful fish filleting.

First up, let's talk about that trusty fillet knife. Picture this: You're all set to fillet your prized catch, but as soon as you make that first cut, you realize your knife is about as sharp as a butter knife. Cue frustration and a fish that looks more like it went through a blender than a filleting process. A dull knife not only makes the job harder but also increases the risk of accidents and injuries. You don't want to be wrestling with your knife, trying to hack through tough fish skin and bone. A sharp fillet knife, on the other hand, glides effortlessly through the flesh, leaving you with clean, precise cuts every time. It's like a symphony of slicing—a thing of beauty!

Now, let's talk about the importance of a clean workspace. Fish filleting is messy business, folks. You've got scales flying, guts spilling, and fishy odors wafting through the air. The last thing you want is to be working in a cluttered, dirty kitchen where every surface is covered in crumbs and grime. Not only is it unappetizing, but it's also a breeding ground for bacteria and foodborne illnesses. By clearing off your counters, wiping down your cutting board, and keeping your workspace tidy, you're not only creating a safer environment but also setting yourself up for success. Channel your inner Marie Kondo and declutter that kitchen—it's time to get filleting!

Alright, now that we're all geared up and ready to go, it's time to tackle the next step in the filleting process: understanding safety.

Safety First

Let's talk safety! When it comes to fish filleting, proper knife-handling techniques and a safe working environment are nonnegotiables. After all, you don't want your filleting adventure to end in a trip to the emergency room, do you? Let's cover some essential safety measures to ensure you stay out of harm's way while you work your filleting magic.

Knife-Handling Techniques

Proper knife-handling techniques are the cornerstone of safe and effective fish filleting. Picture this: You've got your sharp fillet knife in hand, ready to tackle that fish like a seasoned pro. But hold your horses—before you start slicing and dicing, let's go over some essential knife-handling tips to ensure you stay safe and make clean, precise cuts every time.

First things first, always hold the knife securely with a firm grip. You want to have full control over the knife at all times, so make sure your fingers are wrapped firmly around the handle. Keep your grip steady and comfortable, but avoid gripping the knife too tightly, as this can lead to hand fatigue and decreased control.

Now, let's talk about finger placement. Your fingers should be well away from the blade at all times—no exceptions. Keep your guiding hand positioned firmly on the handle, with your thumb resting on the spine of the blade for added stability. Your other hand should be used to support the fish as you make your cuts, but always keep your fingers curled under to avoid any accidental slips.

When it comes to making cuts, keep your movements controlled and deliberate. Avoid any sudden jerks or twists that could cause the knife to slip or veer off course. Instead, use smooth, fluid motions to guide the knife through the fish, letting the sharp blade do the work for you. And remember, there's no need to exert unnecessary force—let the sharpness of the knife and the weight of your hand do the heavy lifting.

Lastly, always maintain a clear line of sight while you work. Keep your eyes focused on the task at hand, paying close attention to the position of your fingers and the trajectory of the knife. And if you ever feel unsure or uncomfortable, don't hesitate to take a step back and reassess. Your safety is paramount, so always err on the side of caution.

By following these proper knife-handling techniques, you'll not only stay safe but also ensure that your filleting process goes smoothly and efficiently.

Nonslip Cutting Board

Let's say you're in the midst of filleting a gorgeous fish when suddenly your cutting board decides to take a little trip across the kitchen counter—definitely not the kind of adventure you signed up for!

That's where a nonslip cutting board comes to the rescue. These trusty kitchen companions are designed with your safety and convenience in mind. They feature rubberized grips or nonskid feet that create a firm grip on your countertop, ensuring that your cutting board stays right where you need it, even when things start to get a little slippery.

But the benefits of a nonslip cutting board don't stop there. Not only do they prevent accidents and mishaps by keeping your cutting surface securely in place, but they also provide a stable foundation for making precise cuts. Whether you're slicing through delicate fillets or dicing up veggies for a side dish, having a cutting board that stays put makes the whole process smoother and more efficient.

When shopping for a nonslip cutting board, look for one made from high-quality materials that are durable and easy to clean. Opt for a board with a generous surface area to give you plenty of room to work, and consider investing in multiple sizes to accommodate different tasks and kitchen spaces.

So, if you're tired of your cutting board pulling disappearing acts mid-fillet, it might be time to upgrade to a nonslip model. With its sturdy construction and reliable grip, you can focus on perfecting your filleting skills without worrying about any unexpected kitchen adventures!

Controlled Environment

Creating a controlled environment for filleting is crucial for both safety and efficiency.

First things first, clear off your counters and create a clutter-free workspace. You don't want any unnecessary items getting in the way while you work your filleting magic. Put away those spice jars, move aside the fruit bowl, and give yourself plenty of room to spread out and focus on the task at hand.

Next up, let's talk lighting. A well-lit workspace is essential for seeing what you're doing and avoiding any potential hazards. Make sure you have ample lighting overhead or invest in a good-quality task light to illuminate your cutting area. You don't want to be squinting and straining to see while you're trying to make those precise cuts.

Now, let's address the issue of cleanliness. Scales tend to fly around, so do this over a sink or a designated area. When using a cutting board, give it a good scrub with hot, soapy water, and wipe down your counters with a disinfectant cleaner to remove any lingering bacteria.

Once your workspace is clean and clear, it's time to get down to business. Remember to work methodically and deliberately, making each cut with precision and care. And don't forget to keep an eye out for any potential hazards, like slippery floors or sharp edges.

Safety Measures to Avoid Accidents

Last but not least, let's talk safety measures to avoid accidents during filleting. Always make sure your knife is sharp and in good condition before you start filleting. A dull knife is not only harder to control but also increases the risk of accidents and injuries. And remember, accidents can happen to even the most experienced filleters, so always stay focused and alert while you work. If you need to take a break, do so—there's no rush when it comes to safety.

So, there you have it, folks—some essential safety tips to keep in mind while you work your filleting magic. By following these guidelines and staying alert, you'll be well on your way to filleting like a pro in no time!

Scaling the Fish

So, you've had a successful day out on the water, reeling in some tasty fish. Now, it's time to decide how you want to prepare your catch. Maybe you're in the mood for a whole fish, skin-on, cooked to perfection. If that's the case, you'll need to know how to remove those pesky scales. Scaling a fish might seem like a daunting task, but with the right tools and techniques, it's actually quite simple.

First things first, let's talk tools. You have a couple of options when it comes to scaling fish. You can invest in a special fish scaler, which is a handy tool designed specifically for this task. Alternatively, you can use the back of a butter knife, which works surprisingly well in a pinch. Whichever option you choose, the goal is the same: to remove those scales quickly and efficiently.

Now, onto the fun part: scaling your fish! But before you get started, make sure you rinse the fish under fresh, cold running water. Rinsing your fish is like giving it a refreshing shower after a long day in the sea. Not only does it help to loosen those stubborn scales, but it also washes away any dirt or debris clinging to the skin. Think of it as giving your fish a clean slate to work with—a blank canvas ready to be transformed into a culinary masterpiece.

Once your fish is nice and wet, it's time to lay it down on top of several sheets of newspaper. Why newspaper, you ask? Well, aside from being an excellent source of news and entertainment, the newspaper serves as the perfect landing pad for those pesky scales. As you start scraping away, the scales will fall directly onto the paper, creating a neat and tidy workspace. Plus, when you're done, you can simply roll up the newspaper and toss it in the trash—no mess, no fuss!

Grab hold of the fish firmly by the tail and as you do it, you'll want to ensure that you have a secure grip to prevent any slipping or sliding. This not only makes the scaling process safer but also allows you to exert more control over your movements. With your scaler or butter knife in hand, position it at an angle against the fish's skin, ensuring that the blunt edge is making contact.

Now, it's time to start scraping away those scales. Using firm, even strokes, begin moving the knife or scaler from the tail toward the head of the fish. The key here is to maintain consistent pressure, ensuring that you're effectively removing the scales without damaging the underlying flesh. Keep your strokes steady and controlled, covering the entire surface of the fish as you work your way up.

As you scrape, you may notice scales flying off in all directions—a sign that you're making progress! Continue working methodically, paying close attention to any areas where scales seem particularly stubborn or hard to remove. Don't be afraid to apply a bit more pressure if needed, but be careful not to press too hard and risk damaging the skin or flesh beneath.

Throughout the process, keep an eye on your progress, periodically stopping to assess how much of the fish's surface still needs to be scaled. Remember, thoroughness is key—taking the time to remove all the scales now will save you from any unpleasant surprises later on.

After you've diligently scaled one side of the fish, it's time for the rinse-and-repeat routine—but don't skip the rinse! Giving your fish a thorough rinse under cool, running water is crucial for removing any lingering scales and ensuring that your catch is squeaky clean. Not only does this step help to wash away loose scales, but it also provides an opportunity to inspect the fish for any missed spots.

Now, onto the flip side. Carefully turn the fish over, being mindful not to disturb the scales you've already removed. With the fresh side facing up, it's time to tackle those hard-to-reach places. Remember, scales have a knack for finding hiding spots in nooks and crannies, so don't be surprised if you encounter a few stragglers.

Using the same technique as before, firmly grasp the fish by the tail and start scraping away at the scales with your scaler or butter knife. Work methodically, moving from the tail toward the head, and be sure to cover the entire surface of the fish. Take your time and pay attention to detail—this is your chance to ensure that every inch of the fish is free from scales.

As you work your way across the fish, periodically check your progress and give the fish another rinse under running water. This will help you spot any areas that may need a bit more attention and ensure that your fish is impeccably scaled from head to tail.

Once you're satisfied that both sides of the fish are scale-free, give it one final rinse to wash away any remaining debris. Now, your fish is ready to be transformed into a mouthwatering meal.

To check if you've removed all the scales, run a finger against the grain of the fish. You should feel smooth, clean skin with no rough patches.

If you encounter any stubborn scales, simply give them another scrape until they come off.

And there you have it—your fish is now beautifully scaled and ready to be cooked whole. Whether you're grilling, baking, or frying, you can rest assured knowing that your catch is prepped and primed for a delicious meal.

Gutting the Fish

Gutting a fish may not be the most glamorous part of the fishing process, but it's a crucial step in ensuring that your catch remains fresh and delicious from water to table. Let's dive into the nitty-gritty of gutting fish, shall we?

When it comes to gutting a fish, efficiency is key. The goal is to remove the internal organs swiftly and cleanly while minimizing any potential contamination of the meat. With a bit of practice and the right technique, you'll be gutting fish like a pro in no time.

Careful Removal of Internal Organs

When it comes to removing the internal organs of a fish, precision and care are paramount. Let's break down the process step by step to ensure that your fish gutting is as clean and efficient as possible.

1. **Positioning the fish:** Start by laying your fish on a clean, flat surface with its belly facing up. This position provides easy access to the internal cavity and allows you to work with precision.
2. **Making the incision:** With a sharp knife in hand, gently make a shallow incision along the underside of the fish, starting from the anus and extending up to just below the gills. Take your time and ensure that the cut is smooth and even, avoiding any unnecessary punctures to the internal organs.

3. **Removing the internal organs:** Once the incision is made, it's time to carefully remove the internal organs. Using your fingers or a spoon, gently scoop out the intestines, stomach, and liver from the cavity. Be delicate in your movements to avoid damaging any of the organs, as punctures can lead to contamination of the meat. If you're uncomfortable handling the organs directly, you can use a pair of kitchen shears or scissors to carefully snip them away from the surrounding tissue. This method allows for precise removal without the need for direct contact.

4. **Rinsing the cavity:** After the internal organs have been removed, give the cavity a thorough rinse under cold, running water. This step helps to wash away any lingering debris, blood, or entrails, ensuring that the fish is clean and ready for further preparation.

By following these steps with diligence and care, you can ensure that the gutting process is executed smoothly and efficiently, resulting in a clean and pristine fillet ready for cooking.

Avoiding Contamination During the Gutting Process

To further minimize the risk of contamination during the gutting process, consider these additional tips:

- **Keep it clean.** Before you begin gutting the fish, thoroughly wash your hands with soap and hot water. This helps to remove any bacteria that could potentially transfer to the fish. Use a clean cutting board and utensils, and if possible, dedicate specific tools solely for fish processing to prevent cross-contamination with other foods.

- **Work quickly and efficiently.** The longer the internal organs remain in contact with the meat, the greater the risk of contamination. Aim to complete the gutting process as swiftly as possible while maintaining precision and care. This not only reduces the chances of contamination but also helps to preserve the freshness of the fish.

- **Minimize contact.** When removing the internal organs, handle them delicately to avoid puncturing or tearing them, which could release fecal matter or other contaminants. Try to keep the organs contained within the cavity of the fish until they can be safely disposed of. If any blood or fluids are present, wipe them away promptly with a clean cloth or paper towel.

- **Dispose properly.** After removing the internal organs, dispose of them promptly and responsibly. If you're not using them for bait or fertilizer, seal them in a plastic bag and discard them in a designated waste bin. Avoid leaving them exposed or allowing them to come into contact with other surfaces or utensils.

- **Final rinse.** Once the gutting process is complete, give the fish one final rinse under cold, running water to remove any remaining contaminants. Pay close attention to the cavity and ensure that it is thoroughly cleaned before proceeding with further preparation or storage.

By following these additional precautions, you can further reduce the risk of contamination during the gutting process and ensure that your fish remains safe and wholesome for consumption. Remember, a little extra care and attention can go a long way in preserving the quality of your catch and enhancing your dining experience.

Tail-To-Head Fillet

The art of filleting—a skill that separates the rookies from the pros. But fear not, fellow anglers, for I'm here to walk you through the tail-to-head fillet process step by step. Get ready to transform that fish into pristine, boneless fillets fit for a gourmet feast!

1. **Preparing your workspace:** Before you dive into filleting, let's set the stage for success. Ensure you have a clean, spacious workspace with plenty of room to maneuver. Lay out your fillet knife, cutting board, and towel for easy cleanup. And don't forget to give your fish a final rinse under cold water to remove any lingering scales or debris.

2. **Securing the fish:** You want to ensure that your fish is stable and secure before you wield your trusty fillet knife. Lay your freshly rinsed fish on its side on the cutting board. You want to position it in a way that allows you easy access to its belly and spine. Now, this is where things get a bit hands-on. With confidence and finesse, grip the fish firmly with one hand, making sure to get a good hold behind the gills or near the tail. This will give you the control you need to maneuver the

fish as you make those precise incisions. Hold your fillet knife securely in your dominant hand, keeping a firm grip on the handle while ensuring your fingers are safely away from the blade. With your other hand, use your fingertips to steady the fish, guiding it as needed to maintain stability. You'll want to orient the fish with its head facing away from you, allowing you a clear view of the area behind the pectoral fin. This is where you'll make your initial cut, so take a moment to ensure everything is lined up just right.

3. **Making the incision:** Ensure you have a sharp fillet knife in hand, like a surgeon wielding a scalpel. With a steady grip and a focused gaze, position the knife just behind the pectoral fin, where the flesh meets the spine. This is your starting point, your moment of truth. Now, take a deep breath and let the magic begin. With a deft flick of the wrist, make a precise incision, cutting down to the spine with surgical precision. Feel the blade glide effortlessly through the flesh, like a hot knife through butter. This is no time for hesitation—commit to your cut and let the knife do the work. As you guide the blade along the spine toward the tail, maintain a steady hand and a fluid motion. Imagine you're tracing the delicate outline of a prized artwork, each stroke adding depth and definition to the canvas. Keep the blade parallel to the cutting board, ensuring a clean, even cut that preserves the integrity of the fillet. And remember, practice makes perfect. Don't be discouraged if your first attempts aren't flawless—filleting is as much an art as it is a science, and mastery comes with time and experience.

4. **Removing the fillet:** As you approach the tail, you'll want to exercise extra caution to ensure a clean separation between flesh and bones. Use the tip of your knife to delicately navigate the contours of the fish's spine, gently teasing the fillet away with each careful stroke. Take your time with this step, savoring the satisfaction of peeling back the fillet to reveal the pristine meat beneath. Work methodically, paying close attention to any lingering bones or connective tissue that may still be attached. With each pass of the blade, you'll inch closer to culinary perfection until, finally, the fillet breaks free in one smooth motion. And there it is—your

masterpiece, gleaming with freshness and potential. With a flick of the wrist, you lift the fillet from the cutting board, admiring its silky texture and glistening sheen. It's a testament to your skill and dedication, a testament to the timeless art of filleting.

5. **Repeat on the other side:** Now that you've mastered one side, it's time to tackle the other. Flip the fish over and repeat the process on the opposite side, making another precise incision behind the pectoral fin and working your way toward the tail. With a bit of practice, you'll soon be filleting fish like a pro.

Techniques for Different Fish Species

When it comes to filleting fish, understanding the unique anatomy of each species is key to achieving perfect fillets every time. Let's delve a bit deeper into the techniques required for different fish species.

Flatfish (e.g., Flounder, Sole)

Flatfish have a distinctive body shape, with both eyes positioned on one side of the head. This asymmetry means that filleting a flatfish requires a different approach than round fish. To fillet a flatfish:

1. Start by laying the fish on its side with the eye-side facing up.
2. Make a vertical incision just behind the head, cutting down to the backbone.
3. Slide the knife along the backbone toward the tail, carefully separating the fillet from the bones.
4. Once you reach the tail, lift the fillet away from the bones, keeping the blade close to the bones to minimize waste.

Round Fish (e.g., Salmon, Trout)

Round fish have a more symmetrical body shape, with fins located on both sides of the body. Filleting round fish requires precision to navigate around the rib cage and produce boneless fillets. To fillet a round fish:

1. Lay the fish on its side and make a diagonal incision behind the pectoral fin, angling the knife toward the head.
2. Follow the natural curvature of the fish's body as you cut along the backbone toward the tail.
3. When you reach the rib cage, use the tip of the knife to carefully cut around the bones, separating the fillet from the ribs.
4. Lift the fillet away from the bones, taking care to remove any remaining pin bones with a pair of fish tweezers.

Other Varieties

Of course, there are countless other fish species with their own unique characteristics and filleting challenges. Fish like pike, walleye, and catfish may have Y-bones that require special attention during the filleting process. Take the time to research the specific anatomy of the fish you're filleting and adjust your technique accordingly.

By honing your filleting skills and mastering the nuances of each species, you'll be well-equipped to tackle any fish that comes your way. Go ahead, experiment with different techniques, and soon you'll be filleting with finesse like a seasoned pro!

Skinning the Fillet

When it comes to filleting fish, one of the decisions you'll need to make is whether to leave the skin on or remove it for a skinless fillet. Let's explore the options.

Skin-On vs. Skinless Fillets

Skin-On Fillets

The debate over skin-on versus skinless fillets—it's a culinary conundrum as old as time! Let's dive a bit deeper into the wonders of skin-on fillets and why they're the choice of many discerning chefs.

- Flavor and texture

    o **Flavor infusion:** The skin acts as a natural barrier, sealing in the juices and flavors of the fish as it cooks. This results in a fillet that's not only more flavorful but also more succulent.

    o **Protective layer:** The skin provides a protective layer that helps prevent the delicate flesh of the fish from drying out during cooking. This means you're less likely to end up with a dry, overcooked fillet—a common pitfall in the world of fish cookery.

    o **Enhanced texture:** As the fillet cooks, the skin crisps up, adding a delightful crunch to each bite. This textural contrast creates a more dynamic eating experience, elevating the dish from mundane to magnificent.

- Ease of cooking

    o **Structural support:** Have you ever tried flipping a skinless fillet on the grill, only to have it fall apart into a flaky mess? With a skin-on fillet, you don't have to worry about such culinary calamities. The skin provides structural support, holding the fillet together and making it easier to handle.

    o **Less stickiness:** Fish has a tendency to stick to cooking surfaces, especially when it's skinless. The skin acts as a natural barrier, preventing the fillet from adhering to the grill or pan. This means less frustration and perfectly cooked fish every time.

- **Crispy texture**

    - **Golden brown goodness:** When cooked properly, fish skin takes on a golden brown hue and becomes wonderfully crispy. This crispy exterior provides a delightful contrast to the tender flesh of the fillet, creating a symphony of textures that dance across your palate.

    - **Umami bomb:** The Maillard reaction—the chemical process responsible for browning—also creates complex flavor compounds that enhance the overall taste of the dish. So, not only does the skin add crunch, but it also adds depth of flavor, making each bite a true delight.

In conclusion, skin-on fillets aren't just a culinary choice—they're a culinary masterpiece. With their added flavor, ease of cooking, and crispy texture, they elevate any dish from ordinary to extraordinary.

Skinless Fillets

While skin-on fillets have their merits, let's not overlook the wonders of skinless fillets. Here's why they're a top contender in the culinary world.

- **Versatility**

    - **Adaptability:** Skinless fillets are like the chameleons of the seafood world—they can adapt to any cooking method with ease. Whether you're pan-searing, baking, broiling, or grilling, skinless fillets are up to the task. Their versatility makes them a go-to option for chefs and home cooks alike, allowing for endless culinary creativity.

- **Ease of eating**

    - **No fuss:** Let's face it—some folks just don't like dealing with fish skin. It can be a bit finicky to remove, and there's always the risk of accidentally leaving a few scales behind. With skinless fillets, you don't have to worry about any of that. Each bite is pure, unadulterated fish goodness, free from any pesky scales or tough skin.

- **Presentation**

    - **Aesthetic appeal:** Skinless fillets offer a sleek, uniform appearance that's perfect for elegant presentations. Whether you're plating up a fancy dinner party or snapping a quick pic for Instagram, skinless fillets always look camera-ready. Plus, without the distraction of skin, the focus remains squarely on the beautiful, glistening flesh of the fish.

- **Health considerations**

    - **Fat content:** The skin of fish can contain a higher concentration of fat, which may not be desirable for those watching their fat intake. By opting for skinless fillets, you can enjoy the lean, protein-rich goodness of fish without any extra fat.

    - **Cooking methods:** Certain cooking methods, like poaching or steaming, may benefit from skinless fillets. Without the barrier of skin, the fillets can absorb flavors more readily, resulting in a more flavorful end product.

In conclusion, skinless fillets are the unsung heroes of the seafood world. Their versatility, ease of eating, and clean presentation make them a favorite among chefs and diners alike. Whether you're cooking up a storm in the kitchen or simply enjoying a quiet meal at home, skinless fillets are always a delicious choice.

Mastering the Art of Skinning

Mastering the art of skinning fish fillets is like mastering any other culinary technique—it takes practice, patience, and a steady hand. Let's break down the process step by step to help you become a skinning virtuoso:

1. **Start with a sharp knife.** A dull knife will make the skinning process a nightmare, so make sure your blade is sharp and ready for action. Opt for a flexible fillet knife, as its thin, flexible blade is ideal for maneuvering around the contours of the fish.

2. **Make a small incision.** Begin by making a small incision between the flesh and the skin near the tail of the fillet. This initial cut will give you a starting point to work from and help loosen the skin from the flesh.

3. **Hold the skin taut.** With your nondominant hand, gently but firmly hold the skin taut near the tail of the fillet. This will provide stability and prevent the skin from slipping as you work your knife along its surface.

4. **Angle the knife.** Angle the knife slightly downward toward the skin to ensure you're only removing the skin and not any precious flesh. This angle allows the blade to glide smoothly between the skin and the flesh, minimizing waste.

5. **Work slowly and carefully.** This is not a race, folks! Take your time and work slowly, using a gentle sawing motion to separate the skin from the flesh. Follow the natural contours of the fish, adjusting your angle and pressure as needed to maintain a consistent thickness of flesh on your fillet.

By choosing the right filleting method and mastering the art of skinning, you'll be well on your way to preparing delicious fish fillets that are sure to impress even the most discerning diners.

Pin-Bone Removal

There's nothing worse than digging into a delicious piece of fish only to encounter an unexpected crunch from a tiny bone. To ensure a bone-free fillet that enhances your dining experience, mastering the art of pin-bone removal is essential. Let's dive into the details.

Detecting and Removing Pin Bones Effectively

Pin bones may be small, but they can quickly turn a delightful dining experience into a crunchy nightmare if not properly removed. Let's explore some foolproof methods for detecting and eliminating these pesky bones:

- **Visual inspection:** Take a moment to visually inspect your fillet before diving in. Pin bones typically run along the centerline of the fillet and may appear as faint lines or bumps beneath the surface. For larger fish species, such as salmon or trout, good lighting and a keen eye are essential for spotting these elusive bones.

- **Run your fingers:** Once you've given the fillet a thorough once-over with your eyes, it's time to get hands-on. Gently run your fingertips along the surface of the fillet, paying close attention to any areas that feel slightly raised or bumpy. Pin bones can be subtle, so be sure to explore every inch of the fillet with care.

- **Use tweezers:** Ah, the trusty tweezers—the unsung heroes of pin-bone removal. Armed with a pair of clean, sturdy tweezers, grasp the end of the pin bone firmly but gently. Apply steady pressure as you pull the bone out in the direction it's pointing, taking care not to snap it off or damage the surrounding flesh. Repeat this process for any remaining pin bones you encounter.

- **Check twice, remove thrice:** Once you've removed the visible pin bones, don't pat yourself on the back just yet. Pin bones have a knack for playing hide-and-seek, so it's essential to double-check your work. Give the fillet another thorough inspection, running your fingers over its surface to ensure you haven't missed any lurking bones. Remember, it's better to be safe than sorry when it comes to bone-free fillets!

By following these steps and mastering the art of pin-bone removal, you'll ensure that every bite of your fish fillet is smooth, tender, and free from any unwelcome surprises.

Enhancing the Dining Experience by Eliminating Small Bones

Ensuring a bone-free fillet isn't just about appearances—it's about crafting an enjoyable dining experience for everyone at the table. Picture this: you've lovingly prepared a sumptuous seafood dinner, only to have the culinary magic interrupted by an unexpected crunch of a tiny bone. It's a mood killer, to say the least.

But beyond the inconvenience, small bones can significantly detract from the texture and flavor of the fish. Imagine savoring a tender, succulent bite, only to encounter an unexpected crunch that throws off the entire taste experience. It's like hitting a pothole on a smooth road trip—it disrupts the journey and leaves you feeling unsatisfied.

Moreover, small bones pose a real choking hazard, especially for young children or elderly diners. Accidentally swallowing a bone can turn a pleasant meal into a frightening ordeal, potentially leading to discomfort or even injury.

By taking the time to meticulously remove pin bones from your fillets, you're not just ensuring a visually appealing dish—you're also safeguarding the enjoyment and safety of everyone who sits down to dine with you. It's a small yet essential step that demonstrates your commitment to quality and consideration for your guests' well-being.

So, the next time you're filleting a fish, remember the importance of eliminating those pesky pin bones. Your efforts will be rewarded with smoother, more satisfying dining experiences and grateful smiles from your fellow seafood enthusiasts.

Steaking Larger Fish

Alright, let's dive into the world of steaking larger fish! When it comes to showcasing the texture and flavor of hefty catches like tuna or swordfish, steaks are the way to go. These thick, hearty cuts are perfect for grilling, broiling, or even pan-searing, allowing you to lock in moisture and create a deliciously charred exterior. So, how do you turn a massive fish into mouthwatering steaks? Let's break it down.

Method for Creating Steaks

Creating fish steaks is a culinary art form that requires precision and skill. Let's explore the step-by-step method for transforming a whole fish into succulent, flavorful steaks that will impress even the most discerning seafood connoisseur.

- **Choose your weapon:** The first step in creating fish steaks is selecting the right tool for the job—a sharp, sturdy knife. Unlike filleting, where flexibility is key, steaking requires a knife with some heft to it. A long, serrated blade works wonders for cleanly slicing through the fish's flesh and bones, ensuring smooth, even cuts with minimal effort.

- **Size matters:** Once you've armed yourself with the perfect knife, it's time to determine the desired thickness of your steaks. This decision should be based on personal preference and cooking method. For grilling or broiling, aim for steaks that are at least an inch thick to ensure they hold up well to high heat without drying out or falling apart.

- **Positioning:** With your knife in hand and your fish laid out on a stable cutting surface, preferably a cutting board with a nonslip base, it's time to get down to business. Position the knife perpendicular to the fish's spine and make a deep, decisive cut straight down to create the first steak. This initial incision sets the stage for the rest of the process, so take your time and aim for precision.

- **Repeat and rinse:** Once you've made the first cut, it's time to repeat the process along the length of the fish, creating parallel cuts that yield thick, uniform steaks with a cross-section of the fish's anatomy. As you slice, be mindful of any bones that may obstruct your path, adjusting your angle as needed to navigate around them without compromising the integrity of the steaks.

- **Trimming:** With all the steaks sliced and laid out before you, it's time for the final touch—trimming away any excess skin, bones, or belly fat to achieve uniformity and aesthetic appeal. This step ensures that each steak is a masterpiece in its own right, ready to be seasoned, cooked, and savored to perfection.

By following these steps and mastering the art of creating fish steaks, you'll elevate your culinary game and delight your taste buds with mouthwatering creations that showcase the best that the sea has to offer.

Considerations for Different Types of Steaks

Bone-in vs. boneless: When it comes to fish steaks, the age-old debate between bone-in and boneless rages on. Some anglers swear by bone-in steaks, arguing that the bones add flavor and moisture during cooking, resulting in a juicier, more flavorful end product. Plus, there's something undeniably primal and satisfying about gnawing on a fish bone like a caveman at the dinner table. On the other hand, boneless steaks offer convenience and ease of eating, making them a popular choice for those who prefer a fuss-free dining experience. Ultimately, whether you opt for bone-in or boneless steaks depends on your personal preference and cooking method. If you're planning to grill or broil your steaks, bone-in varieties may be the way to go, as they tend to hold up better to high heat. However, if you're looking for a quick and easy meal, boneless steaks may be the more practical choice.

Skin on or skin off: Another decision you'll need to make when preparing fish steaks is whether to leave the skin on or remove it. Like with fillets, leaving the skin on can help retain moisture and flavor during cooking, resulting in a juicier, more succulent steak. Plus, crispy fish skin can add a delightful textural contrast to the tender flesh of the steak. However, some people find the skin unappealing or dislike its chewy texture, in which case removing it is the way to go. Removing the skin also allows for a more uniform cooking surface, ensuring that the entire steak cooks evenly. Ultimately, whether you choose to leave the skin on or remove it depends on your personal preference and cooking method. If you enjoy crispy skin and don't mind the extra prep work, leaving the skin on may be worth it. However, if you prefer a more streamlined cooking process or dislike the taste and texture of fish skin, removing it is a perfectly valid option.

Marinating and seasoning: One of the best things about fish steaks is their ability to soak up flavors like a sponge. Whether you prefer a simple salt and pepper rub or a complex marinade bursting with herbs and spices, fish steaks are incredibly versatile when it comes to seasoning. Before cooking your steaks, be sure to season them generously with your favorite herbs, spices, and seasonings to enhance their flavor and elevate your dish to new heights. Additionally, consider marinating your steaks for added depth and complexity. A marinade made with ingredients like citrus juice, soy sauce, garlic, and ginger can infuse your steaks with a deliciously savory flavor that complements their natural sweetness. Just be sure not to over-marinate your steaks, as prolonged exposure to acidic ingredients can break down the delicate flesh and result in an unpleasantly mushy texture. With the right seasoning and preparation, fish steaks can be transformed into mouthwatering masterpieces that are sure to impress even the most discerning palates.

By mastering the art of steaking larger fish, you'll open up a world of culinary possibilities and impress your dinner guests with succulent, flavorful creations that showcase the best that the sea has to offer.

Portion Control

When it comes to cooking fish, portion control is key to ensuring even cooking and a consistent dining experience. Whether you're cutting fillets or steaks, mastering the art of portioning is essential for achieving perfectly cooked fish every time.

Creating Evenly Sized Cuts

Creating evenly sized cuts is crucial for achieving consistent cooking and a visually appealing presentation. Here are some tips to ensure your portions are uniform and perfectly sized:

- **Consistent thickness:** Consistency in thickness is key to ensuring that your fish cooks evenly. Thinner portions will cook faster than thicker ones, leading to uneven results. To achieve consistent thickness:

- **Use a sharp knife:** A sharp knife will make clean, precise cuts, resulting in evenly sized portions. Dull knives can tear the flesh of the fish, leading to irregular shapes and sizes.
- **Steady hand:** Maintain a steady hand while cutting to ensure that each slice is of uniform thickness. Avoid applying too much pressure, as this can cause the knife to veer off course.
- **Even pressure:** Apply even pressure across the length of the knife blade to ensure that each cut is consistent from end to end.

- **Use guides:** If you find it challenging to cut evenly sized portions freehand, consider using guides to help you maintain consistency. Here are some options:
  - **Ruler or measuring tape:** For fillets, use a ruler or measuring tape to mark out equal portions along the length of the fish. This will help you ensure that each fillet is the same size.
  - **Cutting guide or template:** For steaks, consider using a cutting guide or template to ensure that each steak is uniform in size and shape. These guides can be purchased or made at home using cardboard or stiff plastic.

- **Practice patience:** Portioning fish takes time and practice, so don't rush the process. Here are some tips to help you achieve consistent results:
  - **Take your time:** Rushing through the portioning process can lead to uneven cuts and irregular shapes. Take your time to measure and cut each portion carefully, paying attention to detail.
  - **Focus on precision:** Pay close attention to detail and aim for precision with each cut. Consistency in size and shape will enhance the overall presentation of your dish.
  - **Practice makes perfect:** Like any skill, portioning fish takes practice. Don't be discouraged if your first

attempts aren't perfect—keep practicing and you'll improve over time.

By following these tips and techniques, you can master the art of creating evenly sized cuts of fish. Whether you're filleting fish for a delicate dish or portioning steaks for grilling, consistency is key to achieving delicious results every time.

Mastering Portioning for Consistent Cooking

Portion control is not just about aesthetics—it plays a crucial role in ensuring that your fish is cooked to perfection. By mastering the art of portioning, you can achieve evenly cooked fish with a uniform texture and flavor profile. Here's why portion control matters:

- **Cooking time**
    - **Even cooking:** One of the main advantages of evenly sized portions is that they cook at the same rate. This means that all pieces of fish will be ready to serve at the same time, eliminating the need to monitor individual pieces and preventing any portion from being overcooked or undercooked.
    - **Consistency:** With uniform cooking times, you can rely on a consistent result every time you cook fish. Whether you're grilling, baking, or pan-searing, evenly sized portions ensure that each piece cooks to perfection, with no surprises.
- **Presentation**
    - **Visual appeal:** Consistently sized portions present better on the plate, creating a visually appealing dish that is sure to impress your guests. Whether you're serving a formal dinner or a casual meal, uniform cuts of fish add a touch of elegance to any table.
    - **Professionalism:** Professional chefs understand the importance of presentation, and portion control is a key aspect of this. By taking the time to portion your fish

evenly, you can elevate your dishes to restaurant-quality standards and showcase your culinary skills.

- **Ease of service**
  - **Efficiency:** When all portions are the same size, it makes serving a breeze. Whether you're plating individual portions or serving family-style, having uniform cuts ensures that everyone gets an equal share without any hassle. This streamlines the serving process and allows you to focus on enjoying the meal with your guests.
  - **Fairness:** Portion control also ensures fairness, ensuring that everyone receives an equal portion of fish. This is especially important when serving larger groups or families, where equitable distribution can help prevent any arguments or disagreements.

By mastering the art of portion control, you can achieve consistently delicious results every time you cook fish. Whether you're cooking for yourself, your family, or guests, evenly sized portions ensure that everyone enjoys a perfectly cooked meal that looks as good as it tastes.

Tips for Uniform Fillets and Steaks

Achieving uniformly sized fillets and steaks is essential for both cooking consistency and presentation. Here are some tips to ensure your fish portions are uniform and visually appealing:

- **Use a sharp knife:** The importance of a sharp knife cannot be overstated. A dull knife will tear rather than cut through the flesh of the fish, resulting in uneven portions. Invest in a high-quality fillet knife and keep it sharp with regular honing and sharpening.
  - **Knife maintenance:** Regularly sharpen your knife using a sharpening stone or honing rod to maintain its edge. A sharp knife not only makes clean cuts but also reduces the risk of accidents due to slipping.
- **Trim excess fat and skin:** Before portioning your fish, carefully trim any excess fat or skin. Not only does this improve the appearance of the fillets or steaks, but it also

promotes more even cooking.

- o **Even thickness:** Aim for fillets and steaks with uniform thickness throughout. Trim any uneven edges to ensure that each portion cooks at the same rate.
- **Consider the anatomy:** Different fish species have unique anatomies that require different cutting techniques.
  - o **Round fish:** Species like salmon and trout are typically portioned into cross-section steaks. To achieve uniform steaks, slice perpendicular to the spine, ensuring each piece is of consistent thickness.
  - o **Flatfish:** Flounder and sole, which have a flat body shape, are best filleted along the length of the body. Begin by making an incision behind the gills and follow the natural curvature of the fish to create evenly sized fillets.
- **Measure and mark:** For precise portioning, consider using a ruler or measuring tape to mark out equal portions before cutting. This ensures that each fillet or steak is of uniform size, resulting in consistent cooking.
- **Practice patience:** Take your time when portioning fish, especially if you're new to the process. Rushing can lead to uneven cuts and wasted meat. With practice, you'll develop the skill and confidence to create perfectly portioned fillets and steaks every time.

By following these tips and techniques, you can ensure that your fish portions are not only uniform but also cooked to perfection. Whether you're serving up a simple weeknight dinner or hosting a special occasion, evenly sized fillets and steaks will impress your guests and elevate your culinary creations.

Culinary Sustainability

Fish preparation doesn't end with filleting and steaking—the scraps left behind can be repurposed in creative ways to minimize waste and enhance sustainability. Let's explore some innovative uses for fish scraps that go beyond the dinner table.

Making Fish Stock

Making fish stock from scraps is a simple yet rewarding process that transforms leftover bits and pieces into a rich and flavorful base for a variety of dishes. Here's a more detailed look at each step:

- **Gather scraps:** Start by collecting fish scraps, including heads, bones, and any leftover trimmings from filleting or steaking. These scraps are often packed with flavor and nutrients that will infuse the stock with depth and complexity.

- **Add aromatics:** In a large pot, combine the fish scraps with aromatic vegetables like onions, carrots, and celery. These vegetables add layers of flavor to the stock and help balance out the fishy taste. Don't forget to add herbs such as parsley, thyme, and bay leaves for an extra boost of aroma and flavor.

- **Cover with water:** Once the pot is filled with fish scraps and aromatics, cover everything with cold water, ensuring that all the ingredients are fully submerged. The water acts as a solvent, extracting the flavors and nutrients from the scraps and vegetables as it simmers.

- **Simmer gently:** Place the pot over low heat and bring it to a gentle simmer. It's important not to let the stock boil vigorously, as this can cause the flavors to become harsh and bitter. Let the stock simmer for about 30–45 minutes, allowing the ingredients to meld together and infuse the liquid with their essence.

- **Skim foam and impurities:** As the stock simmers, you may notice foam or impurities rising to the surface. Use a spoon or ladle to skim off these unwanted bits, keeping the stock clear and free of debris. This step helps ensure a clean and pure flavor in the finished stock.

- **Strain and cool:** Once the stock has simmered to perfection, it's time to strain out the solids. Carefully pour the stock through a fine-mesh sieve or cheesecloth-lined colander, separating the liquid from the solids. Allow the stock to cool completely before transferring it to storage containers. Once cooled, store the stock in the refrigerator for immediate use or freeze it for later use.

By following these steps, you can turn fish scraps that might otherwise go to waste into a delicious and versatile ingredient that will elevate your cooking to new heights. Whether used as a base for soups, stews, sauces, or risottos, homemade fish stock adds a depth of flavor that store-bought alternatives simply can't match. So, the next time you're filleting a fish, don't toss those scraps—put them to good use and make a batch of homemade fish stock instead!

Creating Fish Bait

Creating homemade fish bait is not only a practical way to utilize fish scraps but also a fun and experimental aspect of fishing. Here's a more detailed look at each step of the process:

- **Prepare scraps:** When collecting fish scraps for bait, be sure to gather a variety of parts, including heads, tails, and trimmings. These pieces can vary in size and shape, so take the time to chop them into smaller, more manageable pieces. Smaller scraps are easier to work with and can be more effectively incorporated into the bait mixture.

- **Mix with binding agent:** In a mixing bowl, combine the chopped fish scraps with a binding agent of your choice. Common options include flour, cornmeal, or bread crumbs, which help hold the bait together and provide a texture that fish find appealing. The ratio of scraps to binding agent can vary depending on personal preference and the consistency of the mixture you're aiming for.

- **Add flavor:** To enhance the attractiveness of your bait, consider adding additional ingredients for flavor and scent. Fish oil, garlic powder, or commercial fish attractants are popular choices for adding an irresistible aroma that can lure fish to your hook. Experiment with different combinations of flavors to find what works best in your fishing area and for the target species you're trying to catch.

- **Form into balls or patties:** Once you've mixed the ingredients together, it's time to shape the bait into the desired form. Using your hands, roll the mixture into small balls or form it into patties. The size and shape of the bait can vary depending on the type of fish you're targeting and the fishing conditions you anticipate. Smaller baits may be more suitable for smaller fish species, while larger baits may attract larger predators.

- **Store and use:** After shaping the bait, store it in an airtight container in the refrigerator until you're ready to use it. Keeping the bait chilled helps preserve its freshness and prevents it from spoiling prematurely. When it's time to fish, attach the bait to your hook using a secure knot or baiting needle. Cast the bait into the water and adjust your presentation based on the behavior of the target species and the conditions of the fishing spot.

Creating homemade fish bait from scraps is a rewarding way to make the most of your catch and enhance your fishing experience. By combining fish scraps with binding agents, flavorings, and creative techniques, anglers can craft customized baits that appeal to a wide range of fish species. So, the next time you're cleaning your catch, don't discard those scraps—put them to good use and see what bites!

Enhancing Sustainability Through Creativity

Enhancing sustainability through creativity in fish preparation involves exploring various methods to minimize waste and maximize the utility of every part of the fish. Beyond making fish stock and bait, anglers can employ several other creative measures to ensure that no part of the catch goes to waste:

- **Fish fertilizer:** Fish scraps can be utilized to create nutrient-rich fertilizer for gardens and plants. By composting fish remains along with other organic matter such as vegetable scraps and yard waste, anglers can produce a natural fertilizer that provides essential nutrients to the soil and promotes healthy plant growth. This sustainable approach not only reduces waste but also contributes to the health of the environment by minimizing the need for chemical fertilizers.

- **Fish skin crafts:** Fish skins, particularly those from species with thick and durable hides like salmon, can be transformed into leather-like material suitable for crafting. By tanning and preserving fish skins through traditional methods or utilizing modern techniques, anglers can create a variety of items such as wallets, keychains, and jewelry. These unique and sustainable creations not only showcase the natural beauty of fish skins but also provide an eco-friendly alternative to traditional leather products.

- **Fish oil extraction:** Fish scraps, especially fatty parts like heads and trimmings, contain valuable oils that can be extracted for various purposes. Fish oil is rich in omega-3 fatty acids, which are beneficial for human health and are commonly used in dietary supplements and pharmaceuticals. By extracting and refining fish oil from scraps, anglers can create a valuable resource that has potential applications in the food, health, and cosmetics industries. Additionally, fish oil can be used as a natural lubricant or additive in woodworking and metalworking processes.

- **Fish skin clothing:** In addition to crafting accessories, fish skins can also be used to make clothing and apparel. Traditional cultures have long utilized fish skins for garments due to their durability and water-resistant properties. By treating and processing fish skins into wearable material, anglers can create sustainable clothing items such as jackets, boots, and hats. These innovative garments not only make use of a renewable resource but also celebrate the connection between humans and the natural world.

- **Fishbone art:** Fish bones, particularly larger and more intricate specimens, can be repurposed into unique works of art. By cleaning, bleaching, and arranging fish bones into decorative patterns or sculptures, anglers can create visually stunning pieces that showcase the beauty of marine life. Fishbone art can serve as a reminder of the importance of conservation and sustainable fishing practices while also highlighting the inherent beauty found in nature's designs.

Incorporating these creative measures into fish preparation not only reduces waste but also fosters a deeper appreciation for the resources provided by our oceans and waterways. By embracing sustainability through creativity, anglers can play a vital role in preserving marine ecosystems and ensuring the health and abundance of fish populations for generations to come.

In the journey from water to table, mastering the art of fish preparation, filleting, and steaking is not just about transforming the day's catch into delectable dishes—it's about honoring the fish and the environment it comes from. By equipping yourself with the essential tools, practicing proper techniques, and embracing creativity in sustainability, you can elevate your culinary experience while minimizing waste and maximizing the utility of every part of the fish.

As you venture into the realm of fish preparation, remember that each step—from scaling and gutting to filleting and portioning—plays a crucial role in preserving the integrity of the fish and enhancing the dining experience. Whether you're savoring a perfectly grilled fillet or crafting unique creations from fish scraps, every effort contributes to a more sustainable approach to fishing and cooking.

So, as you set off on your culinary adventures, let the principles of respect for nature, creativity, and sustainability guide your actions. By doing so, you not only create delicious meals but also foster a deeper connection to the world around you—one fillet at a time.

Chapter 5:

Incredible, True, and Sometimes Terrifying Tales!

Welcome to Chapter 5, where we dive headfirst into the thrilling world of unbelievable fishing tales.

But before we get into the details, let me introduce myself. I'm Regan Murphy, and fishing runs in my blood. You see, I come from a long line of passionate anglers, with my dad, Peter Winser, leading the charge. From his early days casting lines as a wide-eyed youngster to his current status as a seasoned grandfather in his 80s, Dad's fishing journey reads like a novel filled with adventure, excitement, and of course, plenty of fish tales.

And then there's my brother, Steve Winser, who's been hooked on fishing since day one. From his childhood days spent casting lines in the backyard pond to his current gig as a professional fishing charter operator on the stunning Sydney Harbor, Steve's got stories for days—and trust me, they're nothing short of epic.

Together, Dad and Steve have amassed over a century of fishing experience, and let me tell you, they've seen it all. From battling monstrous marlin in the open ocean to narrowly escaping the jaws of a hungry shark, their adventures will leave you on the edge of your seat and itching to cast your own line.

These stories will be from Dad's own words and I hope you enjoy them all. So, grab your fishing rod and hold onto your hats, because we're about to embark on an unforgettable journey through the incredible, true, and sometimes terrifying tales of fishing lore.

Chasing the World Record Tiger Shark

The gentle rays of the morning sun cast a golden hue over the tranquil waters of Port Stephens, Australia, as my wife and I set sail aboard our modest 18-foot boat. The air was filled with anticipation, the kind that only anglers on the brink of adventure can understand. With the promise of a new day upon us, we ventured forth into the vast expanse of the open ocean, eager to see what fortunes awaited us beneath the surface.

As the sun climbed higher in the sky, painting the horizon with shades of pink and orange, we found ourselves immersed in the vibrant energy of the Port Stephens Interclub Fishing Tournament. It was the largest blue-water tournament in the southern hemisphere, drawing seasoned anglers and eager contenders from around the globe. With rods at the ready and hearts full of determination, we joined the ranks of those who dared to test their mettle against the mighty inhabitants of the deep.

Little did we know, as we set our lines into the azure waters, that we were on the cusp of an extraordinary encounter—a showdown with a creature of legendary proportions that would etch our names into the annals of fishing history.

The Port Stephens Interclub Fishing Tournament is the highlight of the angling calendar, drawing seasoned anglers and eager contenders from around the world to test their skills against the ocean's largest creatures. As the sun rose over the horizon, the atmosphere crackled with anticipation. Anglers, both seasoned veterans and enthusiastic newcomers, prepared their gear for a day of thrilling competition.

Our boat was equipped with both heavy gear for the formidable Tiger sharks and Great Whites, as well as lighter outfits primed for the sleek Hammerheads and swift Makos. With baits set deep in the water and lines ready to strike at the slightest nibble, we were ready for action.

The air was electric with excitement as we scanned the horizon, eyes peeled for any sign of movement beneath the surface. Each angler aboard our vessel carried a mix of nerves and anticipation, knowing that at any moment, they could be locked in a battle of strength and will against some of the ocean's most powerful predators.

As the tournament got underway, the tension was palpable. Every angler on board was focused, ready to seize the opportunity to land a trophy-worthy catch, we awaited the thrilling moment when the ocean would reveal its secrets and the true test of our skills would begin.

As the hours slipped by, the gentle lull of the ocean belied the brewing excitement aboard our vessel. Then, suddenly, it happened—a violent strike on one of our lighter lines sent a jolt of adrenaline coursing through my veins. Without hesitation, I lunged for the rod, my heart pounding with anticipation.

Initially, I had hoped for the familiar thrill of battling a Hammerhead or the swift agility of a Mako. But as I grappled with the rod and felt the immense power surging through the line, I knew instantly that this was no ordinary catch. The force on the other end was like a heavyweight stirring in the deep, a creature of unparalleled strength and determination.

With every pulse of the rod and every strain on the line, the enormity of the challenge became increasingly apparent. This was no mere skirmish with a common predator—this was a clash of titans, a battle for dominance between man and the ocean's most formidable inhabitants.

As the line stretched taut and the reel screamed, I braced myself for the fight of a lifetime. Little did I know that this encounter would test not only my strength and skill but also my very limits of endurance and resolve.

As the day wore on, the tranquility of the open waters gave way to the raw intensity of the battle that unfolded before us. The 22 lbs. strain breaking line strained against the immense power of the creature lurking beneath the surface, and we found ourselves thrust into a struggle that tested our resolve like never before.

Hour after hour, we were locked in a relentless tug-of-war with the formidable tiger shark, each moment stretching into eternity as we battled against the relentless pull of the deep. Every surge and pull of the line was met with grit and determination, our muscles straining with effort as we refused to yield to the relentless force of nature.

As the sun climbed higher in the sky, fatigue began to set in, but still, we pressed on, driven by sheer determination and a refusal to admit defeat. With every passing moment, the struggle became more intense, the line vibrating with the raw power of the creature at the other end.

For eleven and a half grueling hours, we were locked in a battle of wills with the massive tiger shark, each moment pushing us to the brink of exhaustion. But still, we refused to give up, clinging to the hope that victory was within our grasp if only we had the strength to endure.

As the relentless battle dragged on, fatigue crept over us like a heavy shroud, weighing down our limbs and clouding our minds. Yet, despite the weariness that threatened to consume us, we remained steadfast in our determination to emerge victorious.

In the waning light of the day, as the sun dipped below the horizon and darkness descended upon the vast expanse of the ocean, we found ourselves locked in the final throes of the epic struggle. The handle of the reel snapped off in the final hour, a cruel twist of fate that threatened to dash our hopes of triumph.

But we refused to be defeated by mere machinery. With adrenaline coursing through our veins, we improvised, fashioning a makeshift solution from the meager supplies at our disposal. With a ball of rags wrapped around the remnants of the broken handle, we continued to reel in the massive tiger shark, inch by grueling inch.

And then, as if by some miracle, our perseverance was rewarded. Under the cloak of darkness, with only the faint glimmer of starlight to guide us, we brought the monstrous tiger shark alongside our modest vessel. The culmination of hours of relentless struggle and unwavering determination was a moment of triumph that would be etched into our memories forever.

As we embarked on the journey back to Port Stephens, the enormity of our accomplishment began to sink in. With the monstrous tiger shark in tow, our modest vessel struggled against the relentless pull of the ocean currents, each passing hour feeling like an eternity as we navigated the vast expanse of the open waters.

The sight of our vessel, dwarfed by the sheer size of the shark trailing behind it, turned heads and drew gasps of disbelief from fellow anglers who couldn't help but stare in awe at the spectacle unfolding before their eyes. For many, it was a sight unlike anything they had ever witnessed—a testament to the sheer power and determination of the human spirit.

As we finally approached the harbor of Port Stephens, the atmosphere underwent a dramatic shift. News of our record-breaking catch spread like wildfire, igniting a fervor of excitement and anticipation among those gathered on the dock. We were met with a mixture of awe and admiration, greeted as heroes who had conquered the depths and emerged victorious against all odds.

It was a moment of triumph that would be etched into the annals of fishing history—a tale of courage, resilience, and the unbreakable bond between man and the sea. And as we stood there, surrounded by the throngs of onlookers, we knew that we had achieved something truly extraordinary.

The fish weighed in at a whopping 875 lbs., earning us over 90,000 points in the competition and initially setting a world record. However, upon closer inspection, the 30ft trace was found to be 8 inches over length, and our claim to the record was denied.

Despite the initial elation of our incredible catch, our hopes of securing a world record were dashed upon discovering that the trace exceeded the permissible length. The disappointment was palpable as we realized that despite our monumental efforts, our claim to the record would not be upheld.

Nevertheless, the experience remained a defining moment in our fishing journey—a testament to the sheer thrill of the chase and the unpredictability of the ocean. The memory of that epic battle against the monstrous tiger shark would forever be etched in our minds, serving as a reminder of the indomitable spirit of adventure that drives us to push the limits of what is possible.

While the official recognition may have eluded us, the sense of accomplishment and pride in our achievement remained undiminished. For us, it was never about the accolades or the records—it was about the exhilaration of the chase, the camaraderie of fellow anglers, and the unparalleled beauty of the ocean.

And so, as we reflected on our journey and the unforgettable moments it had bestowed upon us, we were filled with gratitude for the opportunity to experience the wonders of the deep. For in the end, it was not the record books that defined our legacy but the memories we had created and the bonds we had forged along the way.

The Darwin Trip

As the sun filtered through the curtains that morning, I stirred from my sleep with a jolt of realization. Thirty-four years ago, but it feels like just yesterday, there I was, abruptly confronted with the fact that I had reached the ripe age of 40. The weight of that number settled heavily on my shoulders, and for a moment, I felt as though time itself had paused to deliver this sobering message.

In that moment of reckoning, I couldn't help but reflect on the passage of time and the fleeting nature of life. It was a wake-up call, urging me to seize the day before it slipped through my fingers like grains of sand. I knew that if I wanted to embark on a grand adventure, the time was now—before age and responsibilities caught up with me.

With a newfound determination burning within me, I made the bold decision to undertake a daring journey—a voyage from Sydney to Darwin, spanning a daunting distance of 2,560 nautical miles. Equipped with my new 18-foot half-cabin Stebercraft, boasting a robust 120 hp Mercruiser motor, I set out to conquer the vast expanse of the Australian coastline. It was a daunting prospect, but I knew in my heart that I was ready—ready to confront the unknown, to embrace the challenges that lay ahead, and to write a new chapter in the story of my life.

Preparation was key for such an ambitious undertaking. My boat was outfitted with long-range fuel tanks, extending our reach to an impressive 300 miles between refueling stops. Essential safety equipment, including life jackets and flares, was meticulously organized and stowed away, ready to be called upon in times of need. And thanks to the support of Enterprise Marine, we were equipped with high-frequency radio communication to ensure we remained connected even in the most remote corners of the ocean.

With the logistics in place, my faithful companion Merv and I departed from the Manly ramp in NSW, greeted by a perfect day bathed in sunlight. The sea stretched out before us, a vast canvas of shimmering blue inviting us to embark on our grand adventure. And so, we set sail, eager to chart a course into the unknown.

When we left the familiar shores of Sydney behind, I couldn't help but marvel at the sheer magnitude of the journey that lay ahead. It was a voyage into uncharted territory, both literally and metaphorically, where every wave held the promise of discovery and every gust of wind whispered tales of untold adventures.

As we continued our journey northward, the idyllic scenes of tropical paradise that had captured my imagination seemed to fade away, replaced by the harsh realities of nature's unpredictable temperament. The winds off Brisbane were fierce, blowing from the southeast at 20 knots, signaling the ominous presence of a cyclone forming off the coast of Cairns. Suddenly, the tranquil waters and sparkling horizons of my dreams were overshadowed by the looming threat of inclement weather.

At the southern tip of Fraser Island, the wind intensified to 25 knots, adding another layer of complexity to our already challenging voyage. With the cyclone looming on the horizon, I made the difficult decision to navigate over the Inskip Bar in search of calmer waters, despite the treacherous conditions. But as we approached, it became evident that the bar was in chaos, with waves breaking violently about a mile out to sea.

Undeterred by the daunting sight, I steered our boat in close to the beach at the southern end of Fraser Island, aiming for the entrance in a daring maneuver to skirt around the bar. The plan was risky, but with the shoreline within reach, I felt a sense of reassurance knowing that we could quickly seek refuge on land if need be. After all, I had always believed in the seaworthiness of a small boat, especially when speed could be utilized to maneuver through rough waters.

Our journey continued, with Gladstone marking our next stop along the way. Navigating through the narrows, sheltered by the protective embrace of Curtis Island, we sought respite in one of the secluded creeks for the night. It was here, amidst the tranquil beauty of the secluded waterway, that an unexpected encounter tested my ethical resolve.

As I dropped anchor and prepared to settle in for the evening, I noticed a crab pot floating nearby, its contents tantalizingly obscured beneath the surface. Curiosity getting the better of me, I couldn't resist investigating further, only to discover a sizable mud crab trapped within. Caught in a moral dilemma, I grappled with the ethical implications of taking what wasn't rightfully mine.

Ultimately, after much internal debate, I made the decision to release the crab, replacing it with a $10 note tucked inside a bottle. It was a small gesture, perhaps, but one that eased my conscience and added a touch of humor to an otherwise tense situation. And as we sat down to enjoy our meal that evening, I couldn't help but feel a sense of satisfaction knowing that we had chosen the path of integrity, even in the face of temptation.

As we pressed onward, battling against the relentless winds and heavy rain, our fuel consumption soared, draining our reserves faster than anticipated. By the time we reached Mackay, the weather had taken a turn for the worse, shrouding the coastline in a veil of mist and driving rain. Despite the inclement conditions, we pressed on, determined to reach our next destination: Brampton Island.

Arriving at Brampton Island, weary from days of camping on the boat, we eagerly embraced the promise of a beachfront unit and a night of luxury. But our dreams of rest and relaxation were shattered the following morning when the manager delivered the shocking news: our boat had sunk during the night.

Roused from our sleep by the unsettling revelation we enlisted the help of the island's tractor to haul our waterlogged vessel onto the beach. It was a disheartening sight, to see our prized boat marooned and damaged, a casualty of the unforgiving sea.

Upon closer inspection, we discovered the source of the problem—a crack in the hull at the waterline, caused by an unseen obstacle that had collided with the bow shoulder. What I had initially dismissed as the result of heavy rain and constant bilge pump usage now revealed itself as a more serious issue, one that required immediate attention.

Thankfully, help was at hand, with Bruce Steber sending a skilled repairman to mend the damaged hull. And with the motor largely unscathed, save for a few minor adjustments, we were soon back on course, our spirits buoyed by the prospect of smoother sailing ahead.

With the winds now at our backs, our journey resumed, the coastline slipping by in a blur of green and blue. Fuel stops at Cairns and Cooktown provided much-needed respite, offering a brief glimpse of civilization before plunging back into the vast expanse of the open sea.

As we ventured farther north, the landscape grew increasingly remote and desolate, civilization fading into the distance like a distant memory. Fuel consumption became a pressing concern, compounded by the unpredictable sea conditions left in the wake of the recent cyclone. But despite the challenges that lay ahead, we pressed on, buoyed by the knowledge that each mile brought us closer to our destination.

As the days turned into weeks and the coastline stretched ever onward, we found solace in the rhythm of the waves and the vast expanse of sky above. Though the journey was fraught with uncertainty and peril, there was a beauty in the simplicity of our existence, a freedom found only in the boundless wilderness of the open ocean.

As we neared the south end of Lloyd Bay, our fuel gauge hovered precariously close to empty, a stark reminder of the challenges that lay ahead. But just when it seemed like we were running on fumes, a beacon of hope appeared on the horizon: the buildings of the Lockhart River mission.

Relief washed over us as we guided our boat into the choppy bay, the promise of fuel and respite from the relentless winds driving us forward. But as we drew closer, it became apparent that all was not as it seemed.

The mission, once a bustling hub of activity, now stood deserted and forlorn, its empty buildings a testament to the passage of time. Undeterred, we pressed on, our hopes of refueling dashed by the sight of empty fuel drums scattered haphazardly around the compound.

With darkness descending and our options dwindling, we had no choice but to make the best of a bad situation. We secured the boat with makeshift anchors, the waves tossing it about like a child's toy, and ventured ashore in search of shelter for the night.

Inside one of the abandoned buildings, we found a modicum of comfort amid the desolation. Exhausted from our long journey and the trials of the day, we settled down for the night, our bodies weary but our spirits undaunted by the challenges that lay ahead.

As the clock struck midnight, I was roused from my fitful sleep by the howling of the wind and the drumming of rain against the windows. Stepping outside, I was greeted by a scene of chaos: the wind had intensified to a ferocious 30 knots, driving the rain sideways and whipping the sea into a frenzy.

With a sinking feeling in my gut, I hurried down to the shore to check on the boat, only to find it slowly dragging its anchors, at the mercy of the relentless eastward wind. In the darkness, with the rain lashing down and the waves crashing against the shore, it was a scene of utter chaos.

Realizing that the situation was rapidly deteriorating, we knew we had to act fast. But with the dinghy rendered useless by the tumultuous sea and the boat pitching and rolling in the surf, our options were limited.

In the end, we made the difficult decision to wait for the boat to drift ashore, hoping that we could salvage the situation once it hit the beach. But as fate would have it, our plans were foiled by a small outcrop of coral rock just beneath the surface, unseen in the darkness.

With a sickening crunch, the boat collided with the hidden obstacle, the impact tearing through the hull and leaving us stranded in the midst of the storm. There was nothing we could do but wait for the first light of dawn, praying that help would come soon.

With heavy hearts and a sense of trepidation, we set out on foot, trudging through the dense Australian bush in search of help. Every rustle of the leaves and snap of a twig set our nerves on edge, as we were acutely aware of the dangers lurking in the wilderness around us.

As we made our way deeper into the heart of the bush, we couldn't shake the feeling of being watched, the knowledge that at any moment, we could come face to face with one of the deadly inhabitants of this untamed land. The thought of encountering a Taipan snake or stumbling upon a nest of crocodiles sent shivers down our spines, and we kept a wary eye on our surroundings at all times.

That night, as we made camp beneath the star-studded sky, the eerie silence of the bush was broken only by the haunting coughs of crocodiles in the nearby mangroves. It was a sound that sent a chill down our spines, a stark reminder of the perilous world we found ourselves in.

The next day, as we approached the Lockhart River, our hopes of finding a bridge were dashed. With no way to safely cross the treacherous waters teeming with crocodiles, we were faced with a dilemma. Though I was a strong swimmer, the sight of crocodile slides on the muddy banks left me feeling uneasy, my resolve wavering in the face of such a formidable adversary.

In the end, we made the difficult decision to turn back, retracing our steps through the bush to the safety of our stranded boat. It was a humbling experience, a stark reminder of the awesome power of nature and our own vulnerability in the face of its wrath.

As we waited anxiously for rescue, our hopes soared with each passing boat and plane. But time stretched on, and our optimism began to wane as day turned into night, and still, no help arrived. With each passing hour, the wind howled relentlessly, whipping up the waves and rattling our nerves.

Determined not to give up hope, we made the most of our time on the beach, salvaging whatever supplies we could find from the wreckage of our boat. A battery, spotlight, smoke flares, and rocket flares became our lifeline, our only means of signaling for help in the vast expanse of the ocean.

In a stroke of desperation, I decided to send out a message in Morse code using the spotlight, hoping against hope that someone, somewhere, would see our distress call and come to our aid. "SOS boat crew OK," the beams of light spilled out into the darkness, a silent plea for salvation in a sea of uncertainty.

Days turned into nights, and still, we waited, our spirits flagging as each passing vessel failed to heed our desperate signals. But then, one fateful night, a glimmer of hope appeared on the horizon—a mast headlight, bobbing out in the channel like a beacon of salvation.

With renewed determination, I set to work, flashing out our distress call in Morse code once more, praying that this time, someone would answer our call. But as the minutes ticked by, it became increasingly clear that our efforts were in vain.

Frustrated and on the verge of despair, I made a bold decision—reaching for the rocket flares, I lit them one by one, sending them soaring into the night sky in a dazzling display of light and sound. It was a desperate gambit, a final act of defiance against the cruel whims of fate.

And then, as if by some miracle, the darkness was shattered by the brilliant glow of lights on the horizon. It wasn't just a boat—it was a ship, a massive vessel looming out of the darkness like a guardian angel.

Relief washed over us like a tidal wave as the ship drew nearer, its crew springing into action. In that moment, we knew that our ordeal was finally at an end, and that we would soon be safe and sound, surrounded by the warmth and comfort of civilization once more.

As the boat drew closer, my heart raced with a mix of relief and apprehension. An Aldis lamp blinked in our direction, but the signal was too rapid for me to decipher. My nerves were on edge, wary of another mishap after the ordeal with our own boat.

As the vessel approached the shore, a searchlight illuminated the scene, casting long shadows in the darkness. I waded out into the water, shouting for them to turn back, but my cries were met with a chorus of shouts echoing back at me.

Then, to my astonishment, I realized that the approaching craft was no ordinary boat—it was an army duck, its massive wheels churning up sand as it powered forward. I turned to flee, scrambling back onto the safety of the beach.

The army duck came to a halt, and a group of uniformed men emerged, their expressions a mix of concern and determination. It was then that I realized the enormity of the situation—the ship that had come to our rescue was none other than the Cape Dawn, the marine department service vessel responsible for maintaining navigation lights in the treacherous waters of the Barrier Reef channels.

I learned that they had initially disregarded our SOS signals, dismissing them as false alarms common from land. It was only when they saw the flare signals that they realized the gravity of our situation and sprung into action.

With gratitude in my heart, I thanked the crew for their timely intervention. We were quickly taken aboard the Cape Dawn, where we received warm blankets, hot meals, and medical attention for our minor injuries.

As the ship made its way back to Cooktown, I couldn't help but reflect on the sheer luck that had led us to safety. It was a stark reminder of the unpredictable and unforgiving nature of the sea, and the importance of being prepared for whatever challenges it might throw our way.

And so, with a newfound appreciation for the power of teamwork and the kindness of strangers, we sailed back to civilization and back home to Sydney, our harrowing adventure forever etched into our memories as a testament to the resilience of the human spirit in the face of adversity.

As we started on the second attempt of our journey a month later, there was a sense of determination driving us forward. Despite the disappointment of only completing half the trip on our first attempt, we were eager to pick up where we left off and conquer the remaining miles to Darwin.

Setting out again from Sydney in the 19-foot Haines Hunter, equipped with two 120 hp Mercruises, I was joined by Tony for this leg of the adventure. We made sure to depart only after receiving advice from the meteorological office, ensuring that we had a window of favorable weather to work with.

The initial stretch to Brisbane passed without incident, but as we approached the infamous Inskip Bar at Fraser Island, a hint of apprehension crept in. However, much to our surprise, we found the bar to be calmer than Narrabeen Lakes on a serene day—a stark reminder of the unpredictable nature of the ocean.

Our new vessel proved to be perfectly suited for the conditions, effortlessly gliding through the water at 30 knots and providing excellent fuel economy. Fueling up at Portland Road, where we had lost our first boat, we learned of its fate—it had been repurposed for use at the new Lockhart River mission, serving as a testament to the resilience of human ingenuity.

As we navigated the waters, we found ourselves drawn to the enchanting allure of the many islands dotting our path. These small, vegetated cays offered moments of tranquility and wonder, where we could stand silently in crystal-clear waters and observe the marine life bustling around us.

But our journey was not without its challenges. Rounding Cape York, we encountered the formidable currents caused by the massive tides, requiring us to navigate with caution. The tide differences on the West Coast of Cape York were unlike anything I had experienced before, serving as a stark reminder of the untamed power of nature.

Returning to the mainland, we sought refuge at Orchid Beach, just a stone's throw from the imposing Cape York. Anchoring well offshore, we took precautions by dragging the dinghy far up the beach before setting up camp in the safety of the bush. The night passed peacefully, and with the morning sun, our spirits soared as we anticipated another day of adventure.

However, our optimism was quickly dampened when we returned to find our dinghy missing. The relentless tide had risen to unprecedented heights, lifting the anchor and carrying our means of transport out to sea. With the boat now half a mile from shore, our options were limited and fraught with danger, particularly given the regular sightings of crocodiles in the area.

As I hesitated, grappling with the looming threat of these apex predators, Tony, with unwavering resolve, reminded me of the responsibilities that come with being a skipper. It was a stark reminder that, in the face of adversity, leadership demanded decisive action, even in the most perilous of circumstances.

Hours passed as we deliberated our next move, the absence of a decent knife from the boat leaving me feeling ill-prepared for the daunting task ahead. Eventually, spurred by a combination of necessity and desperation, I made the decision to swim out to retrieve the dinghy. Armed only with a tiny kitchen knife, I set off on what felt like a journey into the unknown.

With each stroke, the fear lurking beneath the surface threatened to overwhelm me. Yet, driven by the primal instinct to survive, I pushed forward, each movement carefully calculated to avoid attracting the attention of any lurking predators. At that moment, the solitary pursuit of reaching the dinghy became a test of courage and endurance; seeing that I was now halfway, fear kicked in, and all previous caution was ignored.

Continuing our journey, we traced the rugged coastline of Cape York's western edge, passing Weipa en route to the Aurukun mission. The mission, with its imposing church and serene surroundings, stood as a testament to the enduring presence of faith in even the most remote corners of the world.

Our next destination was Karumba, nestled at the southern tip of the Gulf of Carpentaria. With the day waning, we sought refuge in the desolate expanse of the Nassau River, a place that epitomized isolation in its purest form. Yet, amidst the wilderness, we stumbled upon an enigmatic sight: Outspan, a seemingly abandoned settlement frozen in time.

The eerie silence of Outspan belied its former purpose as a Crocodile Shooters Lodge, catering to adventurous tourists seeking the thrill of the hunt. Now, with its deserted cabins, vehicles and deserted airstrip, it served as a haunting reminder of the fleeting nature of human endeavors in the face of nature's relentless march.

Karumba offered respite and much-needed fuel, but it also offered insight into the harsh realities of life in the outback. We were told it was too expensive to take their goods out so the beds provided a welcome camp and, as the echoes of Outspan's abandoned glory lingered, it was a poignant reminder of the transient nature of human ambition in the vast expanse of the Australian wilderness.

As night fell in Karumba, I found myself drawn to the wharf, a solitary figure amid the vastness of the outback landscape. Turning on the stern light, I was greeted by an unexpected sight: two large prawns, gleaming in the glow of the light. With a sense of excitement, we quickly netted them, and I couldn't resist the temptation to use one as bait. Little did I know that this impromptu fishing venture would yield an unforgettable catch—a massive barramundi, lured by the tantalizing scent of the prawn.

Leaving Karumba behind, we set our sights on Gove, navigating through the maze of islands that dotted the Sir Edward Pellew group. The journey proved challenging, with shallow waters and discolored currents testing our navigational skills. Despite running aground a few times, we pressed on, driven by the allure of new horizons.

Arriving in Gove felt like stumbling upon an oasis in the desert. Nestled amidst barren surroundings, it offered a welcome reprieve from the harsh realities of the outback. Our attention soon turned to the intricate channels of the Wessel Islands, leading to the mystical realm of Arnhem Land. Here, amidst the rugged beauty of the landscape, we encountered Goulburn Island, a testament to the resilience of the human spirit in the face of isolation.

Fueling up at the church-run mission, I marveled at the dedication of those who called these remote outposts home. Their ability to thrive in such isolated conditions was a humbling reminder of the power of community and resilience.

As we prepared to depart for Port Essington, the ruins of North Australia's first major settlement, I couldn't help but reflect on the lessons learned during our journey. From the patience required to navigate treacherous waters to the importance of humility in the face of nature's forces, each experience had left an indelible mark on my soul.

Finally, as we docked in Darwin, welcomed by the warmth and hospitality of its people, I couldn't help but feel a sense of gratitude for the journey that had brought me here. The boat, now bound for Sydney, served as a tangible reminder of the adventures we had shared and the lessons we had learned along the way. And as I settled back into life on solid ground, I carried with me a newfound appreciation for the simple joys of a life well-lived, tempered by the challenges of the open sea.

The boat used on the first trip was lost in Far North Queensland

The boat that successfully completed the second trip to Darwin

A Fishing Trip We Would Rather Forget

The Port Stephens Interclub Game Fishing Competition of '88 stands as a testament to the unpredictable and exhilarating nature of deep-sea angling. As we set out from the bustling harbor of Sydney, Australia, aboard our modest 21-foot vessel, excitement coursed through our veins like a current in the ocean. We were a motley crew, bound together by our shared love for the sport and our unyielding determination to conquer the mighty marlin that prowled the depths of the sea.

The waters off the coast of Sydney are notorious for their unpredictability, and as we ventured further from shore, we knew that we were entering a realm where nature reigned supreme. But we were undeterred, fueled by the thrill of the chase and the promise of glory that awaited us at the end of our journey.

The strike was sudden and electrifying, a bolt of adrenaline that surged through our veins and sent our hearts pounding with excitement. Steve, with the rod firmly in his grip, braced himself against the force of the marlin's pull, his muscles straining with the effort of reeling in the mighty fish. The line sang with tension, the reel spinning furiously as the marlin fought to break free from its unseen captor. For a moment, time seemed to stand still as we watched the epic struggle unfold before our eyes. The sea churned around us, the surface breaking into frothy waves as the marlin surged against the resistance of the line. But Steve was a seasoned angler, his skill and determination unwavering in the face of the marlin's ferocious onslaught.

Steve strained to keep the powerful marlin under control, his hands gripping the rod with white-knuckled intensity as he fought to keep the line from snapping under the immense pressure. The marlin, sensing freedom slipping away, thrashed and twisted in a desperate bid to escape, its sleek body shimmering with iridescent hues in the sunlight.

With each surge and dive, the marlin tested Steve's mettle, its sheer strength and determination matched only by his own. But Steve was not one to back down from a challenge, his years of experience on the water honing his skills. He knew that to land a catch of this magnitude would require every ounce of strength and concentration he possessed.

As the battle raged on, our vessel rocked and pitched on the tumultuous waves, the wind whipping through the air with a ferocity that matched the marlin's own fury. But amid the chaos, Steve remained steadfast, his focus unbroken as he locked eyes with his elusive quarry.

Hour after hour, the struggle continued, each moment bringing us closer to victory or defeat. But Steve refused to give in, his determination fueled by the knowledge that he was on the cusp of achieving something truly extraordinary.

And then, in a sudden and dramatic climax, victory was ours. With one final surge of energy, Steve reeled in the magnificent marlin, its massive form thrashing and twisting as it fought against its inevitable fate. But it was no match for Steve's skill and determination, he brought the marlin alongside our vessel, its sleek, muscular body glistening in the sunlight.

It was a moment of pure exhilaration, a testament to the indomitable spirit of man and the raw power of the ocean. As we stood in awe of the magnificent creature before us, we knew that we had witnessed something truly extraordinary—a battle for the ages, played out on the canvas of the open sea.

The black marlin, a majestic creature weighing in at 103 kilograms, put up a valiant fight, testing Steve's strength and resolve to their limits. It was a battle of wills, man against beast, played out against the backdrop of a vast and unforgiving ocean.

But just as victory seemed within our grasp, disaster struck. Without warning, a monstrous storm descended upon us from the north-east. As we were looking at a 3.5 hour haul back to shore the storm hit with the force of a sledgehammer, catching us completely off guard. One moment, we were basking in the glow of our hard-won victory, and the next, we were plunged into a maelstrom of chaos and confusion. The wind howled, whipping through the air with a bone-chilling ferocity, while huge waves rose up, threatening to swallow us whole.

Our vessel, once a symbol of our triumph, now felt like nothing more than a fragile toy tossed about on the whim of the storm. The sea churned and roiled around us, its dark depths hiding unseen dangers that lurked just beneath the surface. With each bone-jarring crash of the waves, our hearts sank a little lower, the realization dawning on us that we were well and truly at the mercy of the elements.

For hours on end, we battled against the storm, our hands blistered from gripping the wheel, our bodies battered and bruised from the relentless onslaught of wind and waves. Every ounce of our strength was devoted to keeping our vessel afloat, to riding out the fury of the storm and emerging on the other side unscathed.

But the storm was relentless, its fury undiminished by our efforts to tame it. With each passing moment, it seemed to grow stronger, more determined to break us and drag us down into the depths below. And as the hours stretched on into eternity, we began to wonder if we would ever see land again, if we would ever feel the solid ground beneath our feet.

And then, just when it seemed that all hope was lost, a glimmer of light appeared on the horizon. Through the driving rain and the crashing waves, we caught sight of land—a beacon of hope in the midst of the storm. With renewed determination, we set our course for shore, our eyes fixed on the distant coastline as we pushed forward with all the strength we could muster.

And then, finally, after what felt like an eternity, we reached land only to discover we had been blown 18 miles south of our port. Against the weather, we must turn back into the storm and push north for another hour and a half. And then, finally, the sight of land, we were never so happy to see the familiar coastline.

As we stood on the shore, gazing out at the roiling sea, we knew that we had faced our greatest challenge and emerged victorious. The Port Stephens Interclub Game Fishing Competition of '88 may have been a journey we would rather forget, but it was also a testament to the indomitable spirit of the human soul—a reminder that even in the face of the greatest adversity, we are capable of rising to the occasion and conquering our fears.

The standing start of the race out to the fishing grounds for the Port Stephens inter-club game fishing competition

The Little Boat That Slayed Goliath

This is a story in the words of Warwick Anderson.

I chanced upon some information that really got me thinking now that everyone's favorite Port Stevens Tournament is once more there to be fished and won. What tweaked my interest was a glance at the captures made by Brian Bohm at the 1974 interclub that was won by Brian and his skipper Peter Winser on Pete's 18 foot outboard powered Savage "Miss Jan". This was actually a tumultuous result and I suppose the best way to appreciate it was to analyze and understand the circumstances because there might be some secrets there that will help someone towards lifting that wonderful champion boat trophy in 2008.

To say that Peter Winser and Brian Bohm were innovators is a major understatement because they actually up-ended the way we fished. Back in those dim and distant days things were very different as while the boats were either petrol or diesel powered they were generally slow and cumbersome without either the speed or the ability to back down onto fish. Depth recorders were cumbersome with a limited ability to reach any real depths, GPS was unknown, only the very wealthy had an autopilot and fishing rods were long and unwieldy, and the majority of big game reels were star drag from Penn and Ocean City, with very few lever drag reels available.

Few, if any, were fishing the continental shelf well off the coast of New South Wales, and most concentrated on the 60-fathom line or the islands closer inshore. There was no minimum weight on Marlin or shark with many boats fishing light tackle for these gamefish. Additionally, there was no structured tag and release angling and at the interclub, everyone fished for the Champion Boat Captcha trophy with the Golden Fleece Shield as a secondary consideration. Port Stephens itself was vastly different with no marinas or retaining walls at Nelson Bay at the time.

Fishing techniques were also very different and while a few of the more innovative marlin boat skippers were pulling a pattern of Hawaiian Kona heads and knuckle heads the vast majority were still skipping mullet or Benito baits as it was hard to troll slowly.

So, into this tournament comes a little 18 foot long fibreglass Savage boat, powered by an outboard motor with a small borrowed outboard that would allow the boat to troll slowly pulling live baits as per the formula that had been working well for Peter Winser and Brian Bohm out of their home port of Pittwater NSW. Using their slow trolling system, Peter managed to capture a Black Marlin 116 pounds on 12-pound line, and Brian caught a Black Marlin of 158 pounds on 20-pound line and a black-tipped whaler shark 168 pounds on 20-pound line. This may not seem to be all that substantial at today's rates but there was a scarcity of game fish that year and in their efforts to give them the champion boat trophy for the heaviest aggregate weight of Marlin Captured in the Inter Club.

The end result created an uproar, with this little trailer boat winning the most prestigious tournament in the country at that time, and the endeavors of these two Broken Bay fishermen broke new ground in both fishing techniques and the types of boats that were needed to be competitive with all of the big boys. Nowadays, a 5.5 or 6-metre boat really can mix it with anyone in the tournament, and you certainly don't need a large flybridge sports fishermen to bring home the proverbial bacon, and far lower costs have managed to bring many more substantially younger fishermen into our wonderful sport.

The other thing that Peter and Brian did was to teach us all how to think outside the box and just maybe you don't need the frustration of trying to fish the "car park" with 120 other boats when there may just be something else for you to do.

It's certainly worth a thought.

Some Final Sound Bites From the Fishing Legend

Fishing has always been more than just a hobby for me—it's been a calling, a way of life that has woven itself into the very fabric of my being. From the moment I first cast a line into the water, I knew that I had found my true passion, a love affair with the sea that would shape the course of my life in ways I never could have imagined.

As I look back on the countless hours spent chasing elusive creatures beneath the surface, I can't help but smile at the memories that flood my mind. There have been moments of triumph, like the time I reeled in a record-breaking marlin or the unforgettable sight of my son landing his first big catch. But there have also been moments of sheer chaos, like the time a storm descended upon us without warning or the countless mishaps that have left me shaking my head in disbelief.

Yet, through it all, there's been a sense of exhilaration, a feeling of being alive in the truest sense of the word. Because out on the open sea, anything can happen, and each day brings with it the promise of adventure and discovery. It's a world where the rules are dictated by nature, where the only certainty is uncertainty, and where the line between triumph and tragedy is often razor-thin.

But therein lies the beauty of it all—the thrill of the chase, the adrenaline rush of a big catch, and the camaraderie shared with fellow anglers. It's a world where time seems to stand still, where the worries of the world fade away, and where the only thing that matters is the next cast, the next bite, the next opportunity to test your skills against the might of the ocean.

And as I reflect on a lifetime spent in pursuit of that elusive thrill, I can't help but feel a sense of gratitude for the countless memories and experiences that fishing has given me. Because in the end, it's not just about the fish we catch or the records we break—it's about the journey itself, the moments of joy and laughter, the challenges overcome, and the friendships forged along the way.

So, here's to a lifetime spent chasing dreams on the open sea, to the mishaps and triumphs that have shaped me into the angler I am today, and to the endless adventure that still awaits on the horizon. Because as long as there are fish to catch and oceans to explore, I'll be out there, rod in hand, chasing that elusive creature of the deep with all the passion and determination I can muster.

That night passing Scotland Island remains etched in my memory as a vivid reminder of how quickly a routine fishing trip can spiral into chaos. The tranquility of the moonlit waters was shattered by the sudden appearance of a dinghy, its silhouette emerging from the darkness like a specter haunting the night. In the blink of an eye, we found ourselves in a precarious situation, with the fate of our vessel hanging in the balance.

Instinct kicked in, and I made a split-second decision to reverse course, hoping to avoid a collision with the unlit craft. But in my haste to maneuver our boat to safety, I pushed the gearbox to its limits, the engine protesting with a tortured groan as the gears ground against each other with alarming ferocity. It was a cacophony of mechanical anguish, a symphony of destruction that reverberated through the stillness of the night.

When the dust settled, and the chaos subsided, we were left to survey the damage—a gearbox battered and bruised, its once-mighty teeth now reduced to shattered fragments. It was a sobering sight, a stark reminder of the fragility of our equipment in the face of unexpected challenges.

But the real blow came when we approached the insurance company, seeking coverage for the repairs. To our dismay, we were met with a cold, bureaucratic response—"no accident, no payout." It was a harsh reality check, a reminder that in the eyes of the law, technicalities reign supreme, and the fine print of insurance policies can often be our undoing.

Yet, even in the face of adversity, we refused to be deterred. We rolled up our sleeves, dug deep into our pockets, and set about repairing the damage ourselves, determined to overcome whatever obstacles stood in our way. It was a testament to the resilience and resourcefulness of the human spirit, a reminder that sometimes, the greatest victories are won not on the battlefield, but in the quiet moments of perseverance and determination.

And so, as I reflect on that fateful night passing Scotland Island, I am reminded once again of the unpredictable nature of life on the open sea. But I am also reminded of the strength and resilience that lie within each of us, waiting to be unleashed in the face of adversity. It is in those moments of trial and tribulation that we truly discover what we are capable of, and it is in those moments that our truest selves are revealed.

Seeking refuge behind Box Head during another bout of foul weather, a thrilling yet nerve-wracking encounter unfolded when my wife's fishing line suddenly went taut. The immense weight on the other end hinted at a formidable catch, and to our amazement, it turned out to be a whopping 291 lbs. whaler shark—a memorable moment that took us on an unexpected adventure.

Looking back on these encounters now, they serve as a reminder of the inherent risks and rewards of our beloved sport. In the unpredictable world of game fishing, every outing is an adventure, every catch a triumph of skill and perseverance. And while the memories may fade with time, the thrill of the chase and the camaraderie of fellow anglers will always remain etched in our hearts and minds.

Of course, there were also moments of pure exhilaration, like the time I took my son Steve out for a fishing trip and he landed a 42 lbs. wahoo on 13 lbs. line. Those three fish—the kingfish, the whaler, and the wahoo—still hold records at the club to this day, a testament to the skill and determination of a young angler with a passion for the sport.

And then there was the unforgettable trip to Cairns with Barry Kinsela where we landed a black marlin weighing in at a whopping 1,015 lb. The sheer power and majesty of that fish, thrashing and fighting against the line, is a sight I'll never forget. It's moments like these that remind me why I fell in love with game fishing in the first place—the thrill of the chase, the adrenaline rush of a big catch, and the camaraderie shared with fellow anglers.

As I've grown older, my approach to fishing has evolved. I've traded in the big boats and heavy tackle for smaller vessels and lighter line, finding joy in the simplicity and purity of the sport. There's something magical about feeling that tug on the line and knowing that you're connected to something wild and untamed beneath the surface.

But perhaps what I cherish most of all is my membership in the Broken Bay Game Fishing Club and the sense of community it brings. Reading through the pages of Burley Slick magazine, I'm reminded of the shared passion that binds us together—the thrill of the chase, the satisfaction of a well-earned catch, and the endless quest for knowledge and skill.

In the end, it's not just about the fish we catch or the records we break—it's about the friendships we forge, the memories we create, and the legacy we leave behind. And as I look back on a lifetime spent chasing dreams on the open sea, I'm grateful for every moment, every adventure, and every fish that has crossed my path. For me, that's what game fishing is all about—not just the pursuit of trophy fish, but the pursuit of a life well-lived, filled with passion, adventure, and a love for the great outdoors.

Peter Winser

Conclusion

As we come to the end of our journey through the vast and intricate world of fishing, I hope you've found yourself equipped with a newfound appreciation for the artistry, skill, and sheer joy that comes with casting a line into the great unknown.

We started by delving into the fundamental skills that every angler must master—the building blocks that lay the foundation for success on the water. From selecting the right gear to understanding the nuances of fish behavior, these essentials are the keys that unlock the mysteries of the deep.

Then, we ventured into the realm of fly fishing—a pursuit that transcends mere technique and evolves into a graceful dance between angler and quarry. With its poetic elegance and finesse, fly fishing isn't just about catching fish; it's about immersing yourself in the beauty of nature and connecting with something deeper within yourself.

But our exploration didn't stop there. We also delved into the meticulous craft of fish filleting—a skill that transforms the day's catch into culinary masterpieces that bring the flavors of the sea to your table. From scaling and gutting to filleting and cooking, we've guided you through each step of the process, ensuring that no morsel goes to waste.

Finally, we've delved into the realm of incredible true stories—tales drawn from the experiences of fellow anglers who have braved the elements in pursuit of the ultimate catch. These stories serve as a reminder that fishing is not just a pastime but an odyssey—a journey where every cast holds the promise of adventure and discovery.

As you close the pages of this book, remember that it's more than just a comprehensive fishing guide—it's a go-to resource that you can refer to time and time again, whether you're a seasoned angler or just dipping your toes into the water for the first time.

And so, fellow anglers, as we cast our lines one final time and bid farewell to these pages, let's not say goodbye, but rather, until we meet again on the water. May your tackle box be full, your casts be true, and your stories be legendary.

Remember, whether you're battling marlins in the deep blue sea or casting for trout in a babbling brook, fishing isn't just a hobby—it's a way of life. It's about embracing the thrill of the chase, savoring the serenity of nature, and sharing unforgettable moments with friends and loved ones.

So, here's to tight lines and even tighter bonds, to sunsets painted in shades of orange and gold, and to the endless possibilities that await us beneath the surface. Until next time, may your adventures be epic, your catches be plentiful, and your spirits always soar as high as the birds in the sky.

Happy fishing, my friends. And may the waters always be teeming with life and laughter.

References

Albert. (2023, October 11). *Fishing hooks 101: Parts, sizes, types, and more.* FishingBooker Blog. https://fishingbooker.com/blog/fishing-hooks-101-parts-sizes-types/

Allard, T. (2019, September 16). *The fishing basics you need to know to set a hook.* BassPro 1 Source. https://1source.basspro.com/news-tips/fishing-information/7586/fishing-basics-you-need-know-set-hook

Bailey, C. (2023, October 27). *Fishing reels 101: How to choose the right reel.* Angling Sports. https://anglingsports.ca/blogs/ask-the-experts/how-to-choose-the-right-fishing-reel

Best fishing safety tips. (2019). Takemefishing.org. https://www.takemefishing.org/how-to-fish/fishing-safety/fishing-safety-tips/

Burden, T. (2024, January 16). *Fishfinder technology explained.* West Marine. https://www.westmarine.com/west-advisor/Selecting-a-Fishfinder.html

Circle hooks. (n.d.). Maryland Department of Natural Resources. https://dnr.maryland.gov/fisheries/pages/recreational/circle_hooks.aspx

Fishing bait 101: What to use and how to choose it. (n.d.). FishingBooker Blog. https://fishingbooker.com/blog/fishing-bait-101/

Fishing knots for beginners. (n.d.). Calcutta Outdoors. https://www.calcuttaoutdoors.com/blogs/news-1/fishing-knots-for-beginners

Fishing licenses and regulations. (n.d.). AmericaGoFishing. https://www.americagofishing.com/fishing/fishing-licenses-and-regulations.html

How to choose a fishing reel to match rod. (n.d.). RBFF. https://www.takemefishing.org/how-to-fish/fishing-gear-and-tackle/how-to-choose-a-fishing-reel/

How to choose the right fishing rod. (2023, May 19). The Tackle Box. https://tacklebox.co.uk/how-to-choose-the-right-fishing-rod/

McNally, B. (2023, May 2). *How to pick the right kind of fishing line*. Outdoor Life. https://www.outdoorlife.com/how-to-pick-right-kind-fishing-line/

Sealock, J. (2022, September 1). *How to tie a loop knot*. Wired2Fish. https://www.wired2fish.com/fishing-knots/how-to-tie-a-loop-knot

10 deep sea fishing tips for beginners. (n.d.). Discover Boating. https://www.discoverboating.com/resources/10-deep-sea-fishing-tips-for-beginners

Tips on how to set a hook effectively. (2021). Takemefishing.org. https://www.takemefishing.org/how-to-fish/how-to-catch-fish/how-to-set-the-hook/

Watch, O. (2016, June 16). *Fishing: Minimise stress and physical damage*. Ocean Watch. https://www.oceanwatch.org.au/uncategorized/minimise-stress-and-physical-damage/

Image References

ASMR. (2018, May 21). *Raw salmon steak* [Image]. iStock. https://www.istockphoto.com/photo/raw-salmon-steak-gm958307950-261675302

Bloom, K. (2022, July 2). *Man fishing off promenade rocks* [Image]. iStock. https://www.istockphoto.com/photo/man-fishing-off-promenade-rocks-gm1406207916-457845545

Grandriver. (2009, June 8). *Ocean fishing reels on a boat* [Image]. iStock. https://www.istockphoto.com/photo/ocean-fishing-reels-on-a-boat-in-the-ocean-gm157481615-9625680

GROGL. (2016, August 17). *Young man flyfishing at sunrise* [Image]. iStock. https://www.istockphoto.com/photo/young-man-flyfishing-at-sunrise-gm582310010-99829453

JohnGollop. (2010, August 27). *Old fishing flies* [Image]. iStock. https://www.istockphoto.com/photo/old-fishing-flies-gm171150875-14011344

Lifequestint. (2011, March 15). *Fly fishing in Rocky Mountains* [Image]. iStock. https://www.istockphoto.com/photo/fly-fishing-in-rocky-mountains-alberta-canada-gm153216959-15891197

MarceloDufflocqw. (2009, June 7). *Trout* [Image]. iStock. https://www.istockphoto.com/photo/trout-gm149067927-9596944

Mollypix. (2015, August 12). *Fishing for Australian salmon* [Image]. iStock. https://www.istockphoto.com/photo/fishing-for-australian-salmon-gm484105530-71532461

Ossyugioh. (2020, April 13). *Tilapia is an eviscerated fish with a knife* [Image]. iStock. https://www.istockphoto.com/photo/tilapia-is-a-eviscerated-fish-with-a-knife-gm1216701366-354884165

Prill. (2018, April 12). *Various knots on display* [Image]. iStock. https://www.istockphoto.com/photo/various-knots-display-gm945428100-258224681

TammyJerry6465. *Fishermen in a boat at sunset* [Image]. iStock. https://www.istockphoto.com/photo/fisherman-in-a-boat-at-sunset-gm463386609-32685668

Versh. (2023, March 25). *Collection of freshwater fishes* [Image]. iStock. https://www.istockphoto.com/photo/collection-of-freshwater-fishes-isoleted-on-white-gm1472631890-502936743

Printed in Great Britain
by Amazon